RUSSIAN CUISINE

149 GURIEVSKAYA KASHA
161 CRANBERRY KISIEL
182 HERRING UNDER FUR COAT
 (DANUSIA DOES IT)
187 CUCUMBER & DILL SALAT
190 RADISH & GREEN ONION SALAT
203 KOTLETI
216 PAN-FRIED POTATOES
219 LENIWE PIEROGI
225 CRANBERRY MUS

Russian Cuisine

TRADITIONAL AND CONTEMPORARY
HOME COOKING

by Maria Depenweiller, PHEc

whitecap

Whitecap Books is known for its expertise in the cookbook market, and has produced some of the most innovative and familiar titles found in kitchens across North America. Visit our website at www.whitecap.ca.

EDITORS: Caroline Helbig and Jordie Yow
DESIGN: Jan Westendorp, Kato Design and Photo
COVER DESIGN: Andrew Bagatella
FOOD STYLING AND PHOTOGRAPHY: Tracey Kusiewicz
PROOFREADER: Patrick Geraghty

Library and Archives Canada Cataloguing in Publication
Depenweiller, Maria, author
        Russian cuisine : traditional and contemporary home
cooking / Maria Depenweiller.
ISBN 978-1-77050-233-8 (pbk.)
        1. Cooking, Russian. 2. Cookbooks. I. Title.
TX723.3.D46 2014   641.5947   C2014-903227-7

The publisher acknowledges the financial support of the Government of Canada through the Canada Book Fund (CBF) and the Province of British Columbia through the Book Publishing Tax Credit.

15 16 17 18 19   5 4 3 2 1

Printed in China

For my dear family—Olivier, Alexandre, Tatiana and Antonia.

Thank you for being the source of my inspiration.

TABLE OF CONTENTS

Introduction

I WAS A TEENAGER WHEN WE LEFT my hometown of Moscow and landed in Toronto with two big red suitcases. A new chapter began in the life of our family. Canada welcomed us and we were happy to build our new life here. Oddly enough I felt more Russian living abroad than when I lived back in Moscow. As I grew up, my interest in preserving Russian traditions, especially culinary traditions, increased over time.

The topics of home-cooking traditions and culinary history are near and dear to my heart and are of a particular interest to me as a professional home economist. I thought that a book that explores the history of traditional Russian home cuisine, typical ingredients, preparation methods and which shares some iconic Russian recipes might be of interest to those readers who would like to learn more about the Russian culture.

As I was working my way through this book my mother started sharing her culinary memories from her childhood and youth, telling stories about how her mother and grandmother used to cook and what she used to eat as a student. I thought that these little memoirs would help the reader to see some of the foods that I describe here from a slightly different, more personal perspective. I have translated my mother's memoirs that relate to some of the foods that I mention in this book and bring to life some interesting episodes from her own experience.

The recipe collection is split into two parts. The first explores the recipes that were enjoyed by pre-Soviet Russians and have survived through the centuries up until modern time with minimal changes. The second category of recipes is devoted to the recipes of the Soviet era. There are many reasons as to why and how Russian home cooking evolved after the First World War, during the period of civil unrest from 1905 to 1917, and during the Russian Revolution and the civil war that took place from 1917 to 1923. One of the major reasons is that the new government took control of all trade, even small farmers' markets. It was the countless government committees that decided what assortment of produce was available in the stores for sale, what was grown in the *kolkhoz* fields and the quality and quantity of foods that were sold. Before the revolution there was no such strict control.

Food preparation methods changed as people switched from traditional Russian ovens to small kerosene burners and then to gas and electric stoves. This transition affected the time required for food preparation, as well as some cooking methods. The new Soviet lifestyle implied that women had to work for the betterment of society. This transition drastically reduced the amount of time available for cooking and other household chores. So many delicious but time consuming dishes were forgotten.

Smaller family sizes and the transition from living in large private houses into small apartments in high-rise buildings also affected the food choices. There was no more need to cook large batches of food and the lack of storage space for food had serious implications on the evolution of the traditional Russian domestic cuisine.

If the saying "you are what you eat" is true, then I hope this book will help the reader to feel truly Russian for a moment and explore all flavours of traditional Russian cooking with a better understanding of the how and why these recipes became true classics of Russian cuisine.

MARIA DEPENWEILLER, PHEC.

ORIGINS OF TRADITIONAL RUSSIAN CUISINE

USSIAN CUISINE IS A MIRROR REFLECTION of the country's diverse ethnic, geographical and cultural mosaic. It evolved gradually over time, with influences from Europe in the West and Asia in the East. Situated between these polar opposites, Russia formed its own unique approach to cooking by blending different techniques and developing its own.

The ingredients typically used in Russian cuisine (beets, onions, cabbage, oats and buckwheat) are the same now as they were 2000 years ago. While there are more varieties of these nutritious staples available today, the basic agricultural techniques for growing them are essentially the same. Cooking methods have evolved over time with changes in technology and the availability of resources. The recipes in this book use traditional ingredients, but where possible, have been updated to incorporate more modern methods.

Social class had a big influence on the evolution of Russian cuisine, with the middle (merchant) class having the greatest impact on the development of classic Russian cuisine as we understand it today. While the same basic raw ingredients and certain recipes were enjoyed by all social classes, poor peasant households differed greatly from middle class and nobility households in the variety of cooking tools used and the availability and complexity of cooking methods.

Poor peasant households were limited in the choice of ingredients used and relied mostly on the traditional Russian oven and several basic preservation techniques such as drying, pickling, fermentation and smoking (primarily for meats and fish). These limitations created boundaries in the variety of dishes prepared in peasant homes.

Nobility in Russia, since the times of Peter the Great, preferred to follow European cuisine trends, with French cuisine being the most influential. If you had looked at a typical table of a Russian prince, you would have likely found an array of fine French dishes rather than authentically Russian ones.

The middle class—mostly merchants, lesser nobility and well-to-do city dwellers—had enough income to afford a variety of ingredients and cooking tools. Yet, unlike the nobility, they had a strong attachment to their ethnic roots and preferred Russian cooking to fancy but foreign cuisine as their everyday nourishment. The socio-economic position of the merchant class created the perfect setting for the development of authentic and classic Russian cuisine with its great variety, richness and unique flavour.

Russian cuisine has been shaped over thousands of years. However, as noted by William Pokhlebkin—a late-20th century Russian culinary historian—Russian cuisine, in the form that we know it today, was shaped primarily in the end of the 19th century. This was around the time that cookbooks for the general public became available and thus provided a recorded account of foods that were eaten throughout the Russian Empire.

Typical Russian cuisine, taken from a historical perspective can be roughly classified into the following time periods:

Medieval Russian Period	From the ninth to the 16th century.
Muscovian Tsardom Period	From the 16th century to end of the 17th century (right up to the reign of Peter the Great).
Imperial Period	From the end of the 17th century to the end of the 18th century (especially marked by the reforms of Peter the Great, the first ruler to call himself Emperor, and the reign of Catherine the Great).
Late Imperial Period	From the beginning of the 19th century to the beginning of the 20th century when railway systems and other modes of transportation helped regional Russian cuisine reach different parts of the country and gain popularity in new places.
Soviet Period	From the Russian Revolution in 1917 until collapse of the Soviet Union in 1991.

A Boyar Wedding Feast by Konstantin Makovsky, 1883. HILLWOOD ESTATE, MUSEUM AND GARDENS, PHOTO BY ED OWEN.

This painting depicts a lavish wedding feast hosted in the *boyar*'s home. Note that roasted swans were not a rarity and were often served at such occasions.

Medieval Russian Cooking

TYPICAL COOKING TRADITIONS of the ninth to 16th centuries are recorded in the *Domostroi*, a 16th century text that contains household management instruction and advice. Other food records for this period were available in monastic books, providing information on food preparation and consumption. Some also included occasional notes written by travelers from the West. These records provide an indication of the types of foods produced and consumed during this period.

Often in medieval Russian cooking, dishes were based on one ingredient, preferably used as a whole, or minimally processed by cutting or dicing. Before the reforms of Peter the Great, Russian cuisine had a great abundance of simple dishes, however the art of mixing ingredients to prepare dishes with multiple ingredients was not fully mastered, and techniques used for food preparation were fairly basic. Items like salads and more complex multi-ingredient dishes were introduced much later, with the increasing influence of Western European cuisines.

This period produced a number of simple and enduring dishes: kasha (a main dish of boiled grains), dough products such as *pirogi* (baked pies), sourdough rye bread and an array of rich soups.

The most prominent dish dating back to this period is kasha. It was usually prepared from boiled whole grains, such as buckwheat or millet with the addition of other flavourful ingredients like mushrooms, vegetables and meats. The most common vegetables were cabbage, turnips, radish, onions, peas and cucumbers. These vegetables were eaten raw, pickled, boiled or baked.

Another typical old Russian meal was *pirogi* (singular, *pirog*). *Pirogi* in Russian cuisine are quite different from the common North American interpretation (dumplings filled with potatoes and cheese, served boiled and sometimes pan fried). In Russian cuisine *pirogi* have always been a generic name for baked pies with savoury or sweet fillings wrapped in dough. Common fillings were meat (including game meats), poultry, fish, dairy, vegetables, mushrooms, grains, fruits and berries.

This typical Russian cooking style of combining a dough base with different fillings may explain the eager regional adoption of similar dishes originating in Asia, like *pelmeni* (boiled dumplings filled with meat), which occurred around the end of the 16th century.

In the earlier part of this period, rye was the most frequently used grain for making flour, and sourdough rye bread became a beloved food staple on Russian tables for centuries to come. Wheat dough only gained popularity in the 14th and 15th centuries, triggering the creation of traditional baked goods such as *oladyi* (a variety of pancakes), *plushki* (sweet buns), *Kalachi* (soft buns with a special handle attached to the side—see p. 134), *baranki* (dry ring-shaped cookies) and *bubliki* (ring-shaped buns, similar to bagels in shape and flavour, often covered with poppy seeds).

Muscovia Tsardom Cooking

STARTING IN THE EARLY 16TH CENTURY, Russian cuisine acquired class and regional differentiation. Although the cuisine of the tsar and nobility was a private affair, it did have a noticeable impact on traditional Moscow cuisine. Imported goods such as tea, coffee and citrus fruit were first brought to the tsar's court, and only later made available to the general public. Moscow's cuisine in this context is used to describe the culinary principles that originated in the homes of nobility. These principles were preserved relatively well and survived until the beginning of the 20th century in homes of middle class Muscovites.

The metamorphosis of Russian cuisine at this time drew from both the simplicity of peasant foods and the gradual sophistication of the foods eaten by the nobility. For example, the nobility was introduced to the pan-frying method of cooking meats and the use of European-style kitchen stoves. Traditional Russian ovens did not typically have a stove top. Average middle class city dwellers and peasants still used the traditional method of boiling meats in their Russian ovens. During this time, methods of cooking meat also became more type specific. Pork was boiled, stewed or used to make ham; beef was usually boiled or preserved in brine; and lamb and game meats were most often roasted or fried, but very seldom stewed. These methods of preparation were traditional for these types of meats even before the European oven reached Russia.

Culinary habits of the 17th century were heavily influenced by Eastern cooking. A number of Tatar invasions of the Russian territories during the period between the 13th and 15th centuries, and later the addition of new regions to Russia such as Kazan, Astrakhan, Bashkiria and Siberia left a significant imprint on the development of the Russian cuisine. Items like raisins, dried apricots, dried figs, melons, watermelons, pomegranate, lemons and tea quickly became popular, soon becoming traditional items firmly integrated into Russian cuisine.

Cooking of the Imperial Period

FROM THE LATE 17TH CENTURY until the late 18th century, Russian cuisine experienced further changes. Starting with the reforms of Peter the Great, the cuisine of nobility became heavily influenced by Western Europe. It became fashionable to invite foreign chefs, most commonly from France, but also from Holland, Saxony, Austria, Sweden and even some from Britain. Gradually, invited chefs became so common that they almost completely replaced local Russian chefs in the kitchens of nobility.

During the reign of Catherine the Great, Russian menus were infiltrated by dishes prepared using finely diced ingredients. Among them were cutlets, puddings and pâtés, as well as foreign types of soups (milk-based and creamed soups of homogenous texture). It was during this time that *zakuski* (appetizers) first appeared in Russia, quickly evolving from open-faced sandwich toppings to a whole new food class composed of small dishes, served cold, on a separate table. *Zakuski* further evolved from being a minor part of a multi-course meal, to a light meal in itself.

The European-style kitchen stove gained ground in the kitchens of noble houses, especially in St. Petersburg. This brought the adoption of westernized cooking techniques like pan-frying and stovetop cooking. In a way, this was the beginning of the end of the traditional Russian oven, as every new advancement to the noble class was very quickly absorbed by progressively lower social classes until it spread through all levels of society. This process was especially rapid in St. Petersburg where new food trends were quickly picked up.

Late Imperial Cooking

DURING THE FIRST HALF OF THE 19TH CENTURY, French chefs residing in Russia began resurrecting old Russian traditional foods and adapting them to modern tastes and cooking techniques. In addition, they popularized new dishes of finely chopped ingredients like *vinegrets* (a Russian salad that draws its name from vinaigrette), and an assortment of side dishes. The Russian oven and traditional cooking vessels continued to be replaced with European-style stoves and modernized cooking pots, frying pans and baking sheets.

By the early 20th century, the Russian Empire consisted of people of over 100 ethnicities who lived in different regions, spoke their own languages and cooked their own distinctive food. Given Russia's vast territory and multi-ethnic makeup, it is difficult to think of Russian cuisine in a general or unified manner. Nevertheless, it is during this period that the formation of national, traditional Russian cuisine, as we know it today, took root. This process was facilitated by the development of railroads, which allowed access to remote regions. Staple foods from all over Russia were "discovered." Localized items like Siberian *pelmeni* (boiled dumplings filled with meat) and *kurnik* (a *pirog* filled with chicken) from the Don River area became welcome additions to the general Russian national cuisine.

Russian national cuisine acquired such variety, a unique assortment of dishes and authentic taste, that it quickly became one of the leading European cuisines by the end of the 19th century.

Despite the changes and additions to traditional cuisine throughout the centuries, the basics have stayed pretty much untouched. Bread always remained a key part of a meal, and typical characteristics of authentic dishes like blini, *pirogi*, kasha, soups and sweets were preserved. You can explore these traditional recipes in the Traditional Old Recipes section.

Cooking of the Soviet Era

WITH THE COLLAPSE OF THE RUSSIAN EMPIRE, Russian cuisine was hit hard by the Revolution. The old world lifestyle disappeared and the whole meaning of food and eating was revised.

The Russian Revolution of 1917 that destroyed the Russian Empire also destroyed the supply system. Banks, factories and railways were nationalized, and a great number of people ended up on the streets, without food. Those who had the means moved out of the cities and into villages to live with relatives, only to find that there were food shortages in the country as well. Those who remained in the cities were forced to line up outside stores, in never-ending queues to buy food—something, anything that was available and edible.

This period is well illustrated in Russian literature by writers like Arkady Averchenko and Nadezhda Teffi, who, at the time, had very clear memories of what ordinary lifestyles and ordinary Russian cuisine had been like before the revolution.

The Prodrazver∫ka Campaign

BY THE END OF 1918, the First World War was over but a civil war continued in Russia until 1923. The newly formed Soviet government tried to fix the deficit by initiating *prodrazverstka,* a violent campaign of confiscating grain, cattle, poultry and any other edible goods from village dwellers. The government used the confiscated goods to feed the army and ammunition manufacturers, and then sold whatever was left to the common people in the cities. The *prodrazverstka* confiscated absolutely everything edible, including seeds, which meant that crops could not be planted for the next year and cattle could not be fed. The campaign caused a vast number of cattle deaths and contributed to people's hardships.

In Moscow and St. Petersburg black markets flourished—people were selling precious works of art as well as gold, silver, heirlooms and clothes for pennies, just to buy a small piece of bread, if they were lucky enough to find one.

Torgsin Stores

THE GOVERNMENT OPENED UP A CHAIN of specialty stores called *Torgsin* (abbreviated from *torgovlya s inostrancami*, which means "trade with foreigners"). In these stores, people were able to buy luxury food items—chocolate, coffee, caviar, fruit—in exchange for foreign currency, gold, silver or jewellery. However, since valuables were usually confiscated during home searches (which could be conducted without a warrant and were a relatively common occurrence), not many people could take advantage of the *Torgsin.*

During this period a great number of valuable art objects were sold and shipped out of the country in exchange for wheat imports. At about the same time, the Povolzhye region suffered a poor harvest that caused widespread hunger. Within two decades, Russia had turned from being one of the largest exporters of food products to being an importer.

OPPOSITE PAGE: *Down with kitchen slavery! Let there be new household life!* by Grigoriy Shegal, 1931.© 2010, UKRANIAN EVANGELICAL THEOLOGICAL SEMINARY.

This poster depicts the liberation of the modern Soviet woman from old, time consuming household chores such as cooking and laundry, granted by new advancements such as public eateries, daycare for children, factory-made ready-to-eat foods, etc. New lifestyle options meant women were able, and encouraged, to spend less time serving family needs and more time working to benefit Soviet society.

The Soviet Era's Impact on Food

WHILE FOOD SUPPLY WAS A MAJOR PROBLEM, fuel supply was also a troublesome issue. Wood, coal, oil and kerosene became rare commodities. This had a direct impact on the cooking process. Slow cooking, for hours and hours in the old Russian oven, was no longer an option. New living conditions, in communal apartments with limited space, combined with the fuel deficit made portable kerosene burners popular—they allowed for quick and relatively energy efficient food preparation.

Strong propaganda promoted the use of public cafeterias and eateries with the message that household chores like cooking were unnecessary for the new liberated women of the Soviet Union. This propaganda suggested that store-bought, ready-to-serve food was an innovative and progressive replacement for a home cooked meal (viewed as a rudimentary part of the tsarist regime). Asceticism, particularly regarding food, was promoted as the new and progressive view of the Soviet state. Some apartments built during this period did not include any kitchen space. Workers were supposed to eat nutritious meals provided by cafeterias and public eateries with menus approved by countless committees—all organized for the benefit of the Soviet public.

In a setting like this, it was not possible to even think of publishing a cookbook featuring quails with truffles or sturgeon with horseradish sauce. The author could easily end up in jail for promoting a non-Soviet lifestyle. It was nutritional value, measured in calories that the regime prized over taste and aesthetic enjoyment. Food was meant to be caloric fuel for good workers, and nothing more. As late as the 1970s, children attending summer camps were regularly weighed and expected to gain weight by the end of their stay. This was considered healthy progress.

New Economic Policy

HUNGER AND OTHER POST-REVOLUTIONARY TURMOIL were partially alleviated with the introduction of the New Economic Policy (NEP) in 1921. It reversed the government actions of the *prodrazverstka*—instead of confiscating goods it allowed individuals to own their own private businesses. This helped to a great extent in bringing back at least some of the products that had vanished under *prodrazverstka*. However, by this time there was already a generation who had grown up never tasting the Russian cuisine that had existed prior to the revolution. Many people who had knowledge of pre-revolutionary food preparation had either emigrated or died during the tough years. Most of the recipes that survived had been significantly changed with new ingredients, new methods of cooking and a new philosophy.

Collectivization

BY THE LATE 1920S, THE NEP had helped to strengthen the Soviet economy, but this in effect led to a resurgence of capitalist practices, which troubled some members of the ruling party. They worried about "bourgeois" farmers who had prospered under the NEP, fearing that they could undermine the "revolutionary dynamism" Lenin called for. Relatively affluent farmers—dubbed *kulaks* (literally "fist" but by extension a derisive reference to being "tight fisted")—became an easy target, and ultimately a focus of "counter-revolutionary" purges that periodically swept the country. The replacement of the NEP in 1928 by Stalin's Five-Year Plans and collectivization—the process of transferring land from private owners to government led ownership-collectives—had a disastrous effect on the production of agricultural crops. The ownership-collectives lacked the skill and ability to care for land the way the previous private proprietors had. Workers did not care about the quality of the crops as long as they met the quantity requirement, which were set by numerous committees.

The Soviet government strictly controlled what should be planted, and where and when it was planted. Decisions were often made by people who completely lacked expertise in the agricultural field and had very poor knowledge of the local environmental factors that could affect crops. As a result, many foods that were common, traditional staples of Russian cuisine disappeared completely or were reduced in quality.

A good example of this is buckwheat or *pshennaya* (millet) kasha. The traditional preparation called for additional ingredients like mushrooms, pork fat, smoked meat and onions, which were steamed in the Russian oven (see p. 40 for details) for several hours. This recipe was reduced to plain cereal boiled in water with salt, and, if available, some vegetable or animal fat. Thus, a completely nutritionally balanced, flavourful meal was turned into a bland and insufficient side dish, disliked by many.

PRIMUS STOVE

In the early Soviet period many people lived in communal apartments and small rooms without access to proper kitchens. During this time, the use of portable primus stoves (pressurized kerosene burners) was very popular. Primus stoves allowed people to prepare meals in a setting without large stoves by placing the burner on a table top. Primus stoves became an emblem of the new Soviet household. Many writers of that period, such as Mikhaíl Bulgakov in *The Master and Margarita*, mention the primus stove as a typical element of a contemporary household in their works. Osip Mandelstam even published a collection of children's poetry entitled *The Primus* with the first poem describing the work of a coppersmith fixing a primus stove. The image of the primus stove was extensively used in Soviet poster art usually depicting the disadvantages of "old style" home cooking versus the "new and improved" Soviet public eateries and canteens. However, primus stoves remained in Soviet households for many decades. Home economics school textbooks contained detailed information on use of different models of household kerosene burners, including the primus stoves, up until the 1960s.

Modern Soviet Cooking

WITH THE INTRODUCTION OF THE GAS STOVE and electricity in the first half of the 20th century, in the 1920s Russian ovens became almost extinct, and in fact owning one became more of a liability than an asset. With the demise of the Russian oven many traditional foods disappeared as well. However, over time, it was acknowledged that home cooking was still an essential part of life and rather than eliminating this task completely it should be adapted to the new Soviet way of life.

In 1939, the Ministry of the Food Industry of the USSR, under strict supervision by Anastas Ivanovitch Mikoyan (future chairman of the Presidium of the Supreme Soviet of the Soviet Union, the highest legislative body in the USSR), published a book entitled *The Book of Tasty and Healthy Food*. It was designed to educate Soviet people on how to choose and cook healthy meals at home. It was written by expert cooks and food specialists, scientists from research institutes and members of the public health commissariat under strict supervision of the government.

This book became the ultimate guide to Soviet cooking. It did not emphasize Russian traditional cuisine, but rather incorporated a mix of English and French recipes, and recipes from the Soviet Union republics, such as Ukraine, Armenia, Georgia and Turkmenistan. Ironically, this book was far from everyday Soviet family reality and the majority of recipes were impossible to make, due to the absence of most required ingredients. It was a utopian dream of how Soviet food should be in a perfect Soviet world; people were reading it mostly as science fiction.

Just when things were beginning to improve, the Second World War left the Soviet people hungry once again, and food shortages resulted in rationing. The government established a card system where people used tickets to purchase certain amounts of goods. In its rudimentary form, this system survived until the very end of the Soviet Union as *stol zakazov*—a special shop where people used tickets to buy delicacy items, most often canned meat, fish and condensed milk. I still remember using these tickets for special orders—canned goods that were key ingredients in our New Year's feast preparation or stashed away for celebrations like birthdays and weddings. In the 1990s, the card system came back for a short period to ration sugar, butter and some other goods. I clearly recall lining up for over two hours with my mother and baby sister just to buy some more sugar, as the sugar card we had limited sales to 2 kg per person.

The 1950s and 1960s were the era of the *dacha* boom in Russia. *Dacha* is the Russian word for a private summer house where people could grow their own fruits and vegetables on little plots of land. This phenomenon reinforced old Russian traditions of preserving foods for the winter by making jams and pickles. During the Soviet era, homemade preserves and pickles were one of the most reliable sources of vitamins, especially during winter. Literature abounded on how to grow your own fruits and vegetables and how to preserve them.

Russian cuisine went through a difficult time during the Soviet era but nevertheless became an entity of its own. Despite propaganda eschewing food consumption for pleasure, and the strict food regulations at public eateries and cafeterias, home cooking was enjoyed and always considered superior in quality and taste. In general, people preferred to eat and entertain at home. Even the tiny apartments and microscopic kitchens of the Khrushchev era were not an obstacle. In the Soviet Era Recipes section you can explore some of the typical dishes of the Soviet period.

THE KITCHEN GARDEN
AND PANTRY TOUR

RUSSIAN TRADITIONAL CUISINE owes its unique flavours to the vegetables, fruits and grains that were able to thrive in a cold climate and could be harvested during the short growing season. It was also heavily influenced by the richness of the vast Russian territory where wild animals were hunted and a great variety of fish were caught in the many lakes and rivers. In addition, domestic animals were an important source of meat and a wide variety of dairy products. Many key food items used in traditional cooking were, and still are, picked in the wild—cranberries, mushrooms, raspberries, blueberries, nuts, honey, herbs, lingonberries and cloudberries. The seasonality of wild-picked foods gave a rhythm to the cooking cycle, and certain cultural traditions developed around the picking and cooking activities.

The remainder of this chapter explores the major food groups in traditional Russian cuisine.

Vegetables and Fruits

BEETS

Beets (*beta vulgaris*) are biennial plants that produce edible roots in the first year and seed in the second year. Agricultural selection has developed many different varieties of cultivated beets that are used in cooking, as forage for cattle and in the manufacturing of table sugar. Some types of beets are also used for their leaves, such as chard (*beta vulgaris* subspecies *cicia*). Beets come in several colours, from the standard red to white and golden yellow. Interestingly, if you plant a red beet and white beet close together, cross pollination will produce a hybrid with red, white, or a red and white striped root. This striped beet is the best type for borscht, a traditional beet soup (see p. 205).

ORIGINS Beets originate from the Mediterranean and Middle East regions. Old Russia had a trade link with Byzantium through the nautical trade route known as "From the Vikings to the Greeks." It was one of the most important trade routes in antiquity. By using a vast river system it allowed circulation of large cargo ships between Scandinavian lands and Constantinople, as well as access to the Mediterranean Sea and further trade.

Of all the goods transported via this trade route, food items that could not be grown in the north were very important. Typical imported food items included wine, spices and olive oil. It is quite possible that in the early days beets and other plants were brought to Russia via this trade route.

Beets are one of the main root vegetables used in Russian cooking. They are an important crop in large-scale farming and are often grown in private gardens also. Their popularity can be explained by their very easy storage; fresh beetroots can be kept for up to one year in a root cellar. Beets are relatively hardy in droughts, and do not have demanding soil requirements.

COOKING BEETS Beginning around the 16th century, the use of beets in cooking became more widespread. The "beet revolution" occurred during the Napoleonic wars when sugar from sugar cane could not be delivered to France due to the British blockade. France had to quickly come up with a local alternative for this expensive colonial good. They attempted using grapes to make sugar, but the results were far from perfect—the syrup from the grapes would not crystallize and had an unpleasant odor. In 1811, Napoleon was shown the process of making sugar from beets. He was so impressed with the quality of this sugar that he immediately ordered 32,000 hectares be allotted to the growing of sugar beets. Eventually the blockade was lifted and cane sugar returned, but a new booming industry was established, which spread to Russia, and new beet cultivars with higher sugar content were developed. Since then, beet sugar has been a staple food item in Europe and Russia.

CABBAGE

Like turnips, cabbage belongs to the *brassica* family. It is a biennial herbaceous plant with thick meaty leaves that form a "head"—a tight, round compact bunch of leaves. There are many different types of *brassica* plants, such as broccoli, Brussel sprouts and kohlrabi, each varying in shape, size and taste.

Cabbage is one of the most widely grown vegetables in Russia and has been cultivated for many centuries. Regular white cabbage is the most common variety. White cabbage got its name from the almost white inner leaves of the cabbage head. The look of basic white cabbage cultivated today differs greatly from the early domesticated versions as early domesticated cabbages did not have the typical round head shape and had smaller loose leaves more similar in appearance to the mustard plant.

ORIGINS There are several reasons for cabbage's popularity. First, cabbage can withstand harsh climates, which enables it to grow in relatively remote northern regions. Second, cabbage is very easy to store and can be preserved without problem during long winters, providing a good source of vitamins and nutrients. Third, cabbage gives abundant harvests.

Easy to grow, easy to store and full of nutrients and flavour . . . no wonder cabbage has a well-earned place in Russian mythology and folklore.

COOKING CABBAGE This versatile vegetable can be used in virtually all dishes, with the exception of desserts. Light cabbage salads made with vegetable oil, vinegar, some fresh onion and dill are a great source of fibre and vitamins (and can also put you in a good mood). *Schi*, stewed cabbage, pickled cabbage, cabbage cutlets, *pirozhki* (baked dumplings with filling) . . . the list of dishes made with cabbage is endless.

One can't overlook sauerkraut, a variety of fermented cabbage that is one of the most important items on the Russian table. It is made from chopped white cabbage preserved with lactic acid, which is produced through the fermentation of sugars that are naturally present in cabbage juice. It is one of the most widely used methods of preserving cabbage for the winter. Fermented cabbage can be consumed on its own or as an ingredient in more elaborate dishes such as *pirogi*.

Some folkloric attributes of cabbage are not without reason. For example, when a child asked, "Where do I come from?" a customary answer was "You were found in cabbage." This may sound silly, but it's not entirely without merit. Over the years, it has been observed that cabbage plays a beneficial role in women's health and in utero development of the baby. Eventually these observations were supported with solid scientific research that indicated that cabbage is an excellent source of folic acid, an essential vitamin for women of childbearing age.

CUCUMBERS

Cucumbers belong to the gourd family and are essentially immature fruit of an herbaceous vine. Fully matured cucumbers are bitter and not suitable for consumption; that's why tender, young green cucumbers are preferred to older, fatter cucumbers with thick, bitter skin.

ORIGINS Cucumbers were domesticated approximately 6000 years ago and originated in subtropical areas of India. To this day, wild forms of cucumber can be found in some regions of India. Ancient Greeks and Romans knew cucumbers as an agricultural cultivar. It is believed that cucumber was brought into Europe through the Greek conquest of eastern parts of Asia.

In Russia, the earliest written reference to cucumbers are from a German ambassador who left extensive records of his visits to Persia and Muscovy (which is the ancient name of Moscow-ruled Russia) dating back to the 16th century. However, it is believed that cucumber was already a beloved kitchen garden item back in the 9th century.

Early European travelers noted that Russia grew cucumbers in greater amounts and collected much better harvests than other European countries. The same phenomenon was expressed in an 18th century Russian agricultural guide, citing the Russian climate as a key factor in the success of cucumber harvests. Peter the Great issued a special directive to increase cucumber production in the Russian territory, as by that time, the cucumber was already a popular vegetable, among all social classes.

COOKING WITH CUCUMBERS In Russian cuisine cucumbers are often used raw in salads such as Cucumber and Dill Salad (see p. 187). Pickled cucumbers (see p. 73) are also an important cooking ingredient. They are used to prepare *rassolnik* (see p. 91). Plain pickled cucumbers are served as *zakuska* and are added to salads such as Vinigret Salad (see p. 179) and Salad Olivier (see p. 181).

TURNIPS

Turnips belong in to the same family as cabbage and are grown for the edible taproot, which can be round, oblong or flattened. In Russia there are two major types of turnips grown: yellow fleshed and white fleshed. Yellow fleshed turnips are typically the most popular ones with the Petrovskaya cultivar being the most popular cultivar among gardeners.

ORIGINS Much like beets, turnips became a staple food due to the simplicity of their growth and the ease of storage during long winters. Many people erroneously believe that the potato was the main Russian staple food. The potato was actually a relatively recent introduction (mid-18th century) that was reluctantly accepted by the general population. Before the arrival of this novelty tuber from South America, turnips reigned in gardens all across the vast Russian territories.

COOKING TURNIPS Turnips have the ability to absorb the flavours of other foods that they are cooked with. This makes them an ideal accompaniment for roasted and cured meats, soups and other similar dishes. Usually, the outer skin is peeled off and the flesh of the tuber is cut into pieces. Turnips can be boiled, stewed, baked and roasted, and they are usually cooked together with root vegetables such as carrots, potatoes and parsnips.

POTATOES

Potatoes are grown for their edible tubers. There are more than 4000 different varieties of potatoes grown worldwide, and there are many potato cultivars that were developed in Russia. Among the most popular ones are Ogonek, Nevsky, Ilyinsky, Temp and Sotka. They have different benefits in agriculture as well as storage and taste.

ORIGINS Potatoes originated in South America and were cultivated as a major crop of the pre-Columbian Andean people as early as 7000 years ago. They arrived in Europe in the 16th century via Spanish conquistadors. Potatoes were first brought to Russia, as a novelty, by Peter the Great. In 1765 Catherine the Great directed the Senate to pass a law encouraging the cultivation of potatoes all across the Russian territories.

Potatoes were met with suspicion by most Russians. Accustomed to traditional crops such as rye, turnips and buckwheat they were very hesitant to try the new plant. Some people called potatoes "Devil's apples." Resistance continued until as late as 1840, and when the government decided to reinforce the directive to grow potatoes on common lands, resistance culminated in the "Potato Riots" that continued for three years. Despite such unwillingness to accept the potato, it took only 50 more years to transform the potato from an unwanted tuber to a beloved staple food item. Russia's climate is perfect for potato cultivation and its hardiness makes it a very easy crop to grow.

COOKING POTATOES Potatoes have a mild, neutral taste that combines well with many other simple ingredients to create endless flavour combinations. Mashed potatoes with butter taste completely different from boiled potatoes with sunflower oil or pan-fried potatoes with bacon.

Very quickly, potatoes replaced turnips in many recipes. A good example is Potato-Topped *Shangi* (see p. 132). An older version of this recipe would have used turnip instead of potato as filling. Boiled potatoes are a common side dish and are a perfect match for salty *zakuski* (appetizers) such as Russian Sauerkraut (see p. 77), Dill Pickles in Brine (see p. 73), Pickled Chanterelle Mushrooms (see p. 71), herring in brine, roasted meats and other flavourful dishes.

MUSHROOMS

Russian forests are rich with mushrooms and mushroom picking is a favourite hobby for many Russians. Different regions are known for different types of edible mushrooms. In some places, chanterelles are the stars, while in others, boletus (also known as porcini) mushrooms are the main attraction. Overall there are about 200 varieties of wild mushrooms that grow in Russia. For those who don't pick their own, they can be purchased at markets or directly from mushroom pickers. Big supermarkets typically do not sell wild mushrooms, but regular (button) white mushrooms are often available.

COOKING WITH MUSHROOMS After picking wild mushrooms they need to be sorted. Larger and broken ones are set aside for frying. Pan-fried mushrooms with butter, accompanied by potatoes—fried or boiled—make a delicious quick dinner. Smaller intact mushrooms are usually used for pickling, and can then be served as *zakuski*. Porcini mushrooms are usually dried and used in soups. Dried mushrooms produce a rich flavourful broth. In earlier times, especially in northern parts of Russia where summers are relatively short and wet, mushrooms were dried inside the Russian oven. Constant low heat created the perfect conditions for mushrooms to dry properly.

Mushrooms are so versatile that you could cook dinners featuring mushrooms every day for an entire month and always get a unique, new flavour.

ONIONS

There are many different varieties of onions used in Russian cuisine. Cooking onion is the most widely used type of onion. It has a white bulb with yellow to light-brown peel. This onion has a bold pungent flavour and is used in a myriad of recipes. Dry onion peel is traditionally used to colour Easter eggs a deep brown-red.

Green onions (also known as scallions or spring onions) are the edible green shoots that come out of the onion bulb. Green onions may be easily grown in a glass jar on a window sill and are an excellent source of vitamins in the winter.

Shallots are a smaller variety of onions with oblong violet bulbs. They have a mild flavour compared to cooking onions and are often used in light and flavourful salad dressings or as an addition to soups or main meals.

Chives are also used in Russian cuisine. Their delicate foliage has a mild flavour and is often added to salads, soups and other dishes.

ORIGINS Onions were domesticated approximately 5000 years ago and were highly prized for their medicinal properties. Onions were included in the rations of slaves working on the construction of the Egyptian pyramids, they were a mandatory part of the rations of Roman legionnaires and were widely used in ancient Greek cuisine.

COOKING WITH ONIONS Although onions are rarely featured as a main ingredient in Russian cooking, they are an essential component of many complex dishes, lending delicate background flavour to such dishes as *Rassolnik* with Chicken (see p. 91), *Pelmeni* (see p. 100) or *Okroshka* (see p. 97). Onions can be fried, boiled, stewed, roasted and of course eaten raw.

FOLKLORE Onions are an extremely undemanding plant, so they quickly spread throughout Russia and became a staple food. The persistent popularity of this pungent plant is reflected in Russian folklore. Over the centuries, many sayings were developed that reflected the abundance and usefulness of onions as a home remedy:

- "Onion is a remedy for seven illnesses" *(luk—ot semi nedug):* This underscores the usefulness of onions in treating and preventing numerous illnesses.
- "Onions and sauna will fix everything" *(luk da banya vse popravjat):* This saying refers to the two most readily available remedies for treating illnesses from common colds and respiratory problems to rheumatism.
- "In our land, like in heaven you can eat as many onions and rowan berries as you wish" *(v nashem kraju—slovno v raju: luku da rjabini ne priesh):* This proverb refers to the massive abundance of onions and rowan berries as a cheap food source. Rowan berries are no longer used as a main food source, but in the past, these bright, orange-red berries were extremely popular.

LINGONBERRIES

Lingonberries (pictured top, right) are little bright red berries that grow in small evergreen shrubs and are related to cranberries. These berries thrive in the northern climate and are an important staple food in most northern Russian territories. Lingonberries are typically picked in the wild and are eaten raw (their flavour is milder than cranberries), or used in jam and a variety of drinks. One of the typical Russian drinks made from lingonberry is called *mors*. It is prepared by obtaining juice from the berries, then boiling the leftover berry solids with water and sugar and adding the reserved berry juice to this liquid. *Mors* is usually served cold in the summer and warmed up in the winter.

CLOUDBERRIES

Cloudberry (pictured bottom, right) is a herbaceous plant that grows in the Arctic tundra and boreal forest territories. Cloudberries look like small yellow-orange raspberries. They are most often picked in the wild and are an important source of vitamins and are eaten like any other berry—raw, cooked in jam or used to prepare beverages.

APPLES

Apple trees are a relatively common part of the landscapes of temperate climates. They grow in orchards and in the wild, and attract the eye with fragrant white or pink blossoms in the spring. The climate of the southern Russia is mild enough to allow successful cultivation of plums, apricots, peaches and cherries but in northern regions, apples are definitely the winners.

Orchard apple trees require pruning, timely fertilization and special care for branches, such as artificial support to avoid broken branches. Apple trees are sensitive to pests and frost, so growing a healthy apple tree requires some skill.

COOKING WITH APPLES Apples were the principal fruit on both the traditional and Soviet era Russian table. They were eaten as raw sweet treats and used extensively in cooking. They featured not only in dessert dishes like *varenye* (Russian jam), compote and Apple *Pirozhki* (see p. 136), but also in some savoury dishes such as Roasted Goose with Apples and Buckwheat Stuffing (see p. 105). Apples are also used quite often in salads, such as Herring Under Fur Coat (see p. 182), Carrot, Apple and Raisin Salad (see p. 188).

ANTONOVKA CULTIVAR

Russia has many varieties of apples differing in shape, size, colour, flavour and harvest time; the most popular variety is the Antonovka.

The history of the Antonovka is long and complicated and the date that it was first cultivated is unknown. According to records left by Andrey Bolotov—a renowned agriculturalist in 18th century Russia—the identification of apple cultivars was nearly impossible due to the fact that each region had different names for the same cultivar. It is believed that cultivation of the Antonovka started in the Kursk and Tula regions and quickly spread throughout the country to become Russia's favourite apple. Interestingly, the Antonovka name was often given to apples not related to this popular cultivar as a commercial move to popularize new apple varieties. Early 20th century records indicate that the Antonovka was eaten not only in raw form as a dessert fruit, but also used as an ingredient for desserts, such as Apple *Pastila* (see p. 148), marmalade and jelly.

There are 17 to 26 different Anatonovka apple varieties differing in colour, taste and storage properties. Some could be stored without any special requirements, all winter long, while others had to be used as raw material for desserts and preserves. The classic Russian way of preserving apples was *mochenie* (literally: soaking), which involved preserving apples in brine.

A unique trait of the Antonovka is the presence of different shapes of apples on the same tree. Depending on the location of the flowers on the branches, apples may be vertically oblong or more elliptical. Particular growing conditions may be a factor in producing these shape variations.

Grains

RUSSIAN STAPLE FOODS INCLUDE a variety of grains. Grains are primarily used as the main ingredient in kasha or ground into flour to make bread and pasta. The table on the next page provides a brief description of the grains that are used in Russian cooking.

Of all the grains, buckwheat and barley deserve special mention. Over the years, regardless of the time period or political situation, buckwheat and barley were always available as food sources in Russia and could be found in any pantry.

GRAINS	DESCRIPTION
Millet *Proso, Psheno*	Small spherical yellow grains that are usually boiled and consumed whole. Millet can be considered one of the ancient grains as it was a part of the diet of the people in present-day India, China and Korea during the Neolithic period (around 6000 BCE). Millet came into Russia most probably from China via the Black Sea trade route known as "From the Vikings to the Greeks." Cooked millet has a fluffy texture and light nutty flavour.
Oats *Oves*	Similarly to barley, oats are used to produce a variety of cereals, depending on the size of the grain. Oats are used as whole kernels, are medium cut or are rolled into flakes. Kasha prepared with rolled oats is often given to children as breakfast food. Oat flour is used to make blini and to make filling or dough for baked goods (see Oat-Topped Rye *Musniki*, p. 133).
Rice *Ris*	Although not as common a staple as in China or Japan, rice is still an important component of Russian cuisine. Rice is used as a filling for *pirozhki* and *koulebyaka*, as an ingredient in soups and as the main ingredient in kasha.
Rye *Rozh*	Rye is an oblong grain with a dent, resembling wheat in appearance. Rye became popular in Russia due to its ability to grow in poor soil and to yield abundant harvests in a relatively short period of time. Rye is mostly used to produce flour that is used in baking bread. It produces a dark rye bread with a distinct slightly sour and nutty flavour.
Wheat *Pshenica*	Whole kernels of wheat are usually ground to a small grain size to make *mannaya krupa* (Cream of Wheat). It makes very smooth kasha, often served sweet as dessert or breakfast food. Wheat flour is often used to make dough for *pirogi*, *koulebyakas*, *pirozhki*, *pelmeni* and other baked goods.

BUCKWHEAT

Buckwheat is related to sorrel and rhubarb and is grown for its edible seeds. Buckwheat grains are brown and have a pyramid shape. To bring out the best flavour, buckwheat should be roasted prior to cooking.

BUCKWHEAT AND KASHA The word *kasha* in the Western world is often synonymous with buckwheat itself. In Russia, however, it is a word used to describe a main dish made from (but not exclusively) buckwheat.

Buckwheat is a small pyramid-shaped kernel with a brown surface and a white interior. It has a mild nutty flavour. Several types of cereals are made from it that differ by size of the grain—whole, coarsely ground, more finely ground or completely powderized into buckwheat flour. The general name *grechka* refers to the cereal made up of whole buckwheat kernels. *Smolenskaja krupa* (Smolensk cereal), a medium-grain cereal that was once popular but is less so now, is made of medium-sized ground buckwheat kernels.

ORIGINS In its wild form, buckwheat can be found in Siberia and the Himalayas. It is possible that buckwheat was brought from the Himalayas to Russia via the trade route known as "From the Vikings to the Greeks" (described on p. 19). Another theory suggests that it originated in the Altai region of Siberia and was brought to the southern part of the Volga River, where it was cultivated by the ancestors of the Kazan Tatars. This theory has considerable merit because trade relations between northern territories of ancient Russia and the regions along the south end of the Volga River were very strong and reliable.

FOLKLORE ABOUT BUCKWHEAT References to buckwheat as a common staple food and cornerstone of the Russian traditional menu are reflected in folklore. The saying "Buckwheat kasha is our mother, rye bread is our father" ("*grechnevaya kasha matushka nasha, a hlebec rzhanoy otec nash rodnoy*"), puts buckwheat kasha and rye bread on the same level as mothers and fathers. It defines two vital elements of Russian food: not just bread, but specifically rye bread, and kasha, specifically kasha prepared from buckwheat.

BARLEY

Barley is one of the ancient grains that were cultivated by humans for many centuries. It has a smooth delicate flavour and two major types of cereal are made from this plant. The first is *perlovaya krupa* (pearl barley), which are whole barley grains stripped of their outer hull and polished. The name is derived from the visual similarity between barley grain and fresh water pearls that were abundant in Russian rivers. The second is *yachnevaya krupa* (barley cereal), which are unpolished, light beige barley kernels ground up to medium-small grain size. Compared to *perlovaya krupa*, *yachnevaya krupa* yields tenderer kasha with smoother texture. Barley grains are typically eaten boiled whole or are used to make flour and beer.

ORIGINS Ancient Egyptian records indicate that barley was a prominent food staple and a beer making component. Barley was so important to this ancient culture that it was depicted in a specially designed hieroglyph that showed its stalk with grains. The ancient Roman author, Pliny the Elder, wrote that barley was used as part of gladiator rations, giving them strength and energy for the tournaments. Ancient Greek and Roman recipes included barley as a common ingredient and bread made from barley flour was consumed on a daily basis.

COOKING WITH BARLEY Barley was used not only in preparation of kasha but also as a key ingredient for beer, bread and *kutya* (also known as *kolivo*)—an ancient dish with religious significance. This dish was usually prepared for burial ceremonies, holidays related to remembrance of the dead, Orthodox Christian Christmas Eve and the Great Lent. You can try Mushroom *Pokhlebka* (see p. 93) or Barley Kasha (see p. 120).

Historically, barley was one of the cheapest grains sold in Russia, so it is no wonder that kasha made from barley grains was a popular dish through the centuries. During the Soviet period, it was included in military rations as a cheap and nutritious food for soldiers and it gained fame as a typical military food. Unfortunately, ingredients were cut to make the dish more economical, and as a result barley kasha temporarily lost much of its flavour and became increasingly disliked.

SCHI AND KASHA IS OUR FOOD

A popular saying among the Russian peasantry, "*schi* and kasha—is our food," refers to two iconic dishes. *Schi* is a hearty cabbage-based soup, and kasha is a filling dish made from whole grains of buckwheat, barley, oats or other grains. This saying is used to refer to the simple down-to-earth origins of someone, similar to the expression "meat and potatoes" in English. It takes a long time for a saying like this to become ingrained, and the reference to the two staple dishes is an indication of how well known they are.

Meat and Fish

MEAT

SINCE EARLY NEOLITHIC TIMES, around 9500 BCE, people who lived in the Russian territories hunted local wildlife and birds. Game meat constituted an important part of early Russian cuisine. For people who resided in towns and did not hunt, game meat could be purchased from most markets. Game meats were a part of Russian cuisine for all social classes during all periods of history, though it is less common today. Where location made it feasible, nobility could receive game meats as part of the taxes paid by their peasants. Peasants also did some hunting for themselves and used local waterways as sources of fish.

Russians kept domestic animals, the most valued animal being the cow for its milk and meat. Sheep, pigs and goats were also kept. Husbandry of domestic animals in northern regions was complicated by the climate—short summers allowed for only brief periods of time when animals could be kept outdoors. This meant extra labour was needed to harvest hay and build shelter for the long winter months. As a result, beef was always one of the more expensive meats in Russia. Poor peasants could afford to eat *schi* (traditional cabbage soup) with beef only on holidays.

It is important to note that for a very long time, right up to the Soviet period, Russian diet and cuisine were heavily influenced by the yearly cycle of Lents. A majority of the Russian population carefully observed Lenten periods of the Orthodox Christian Church, and meat was allowed for consumption only on certain days of the week. Wednesdays and Fridays were considered meat-free year-round. There were two major long Lents in the year, one ending on Easter, the other on Christmas. During these Lents, not only meat but even fish was restricted on some days. If you add up all the days with meat restriction, it worked out to half a year where people could not consume any meat or even fish.

Historically, the greatest variety of meat was available in the winter. Natural frost allowed for the safe transportation and storage of meats. Winter markets, especially before Christmas, were filled with all sorts of meats: game animals and birds, domestic mammals (veal, beef, pork and lamb) and domestic poultry (chickens, ducks, geese and turkeys). The meat was available in many different forms: whole or in pieces, fresh, frozen, smoked, salted and cured.

All parts of the carcass were put to good use including the organs, which were popular among poorer people because prices were much lower than for other cuts of meat. Intestines were used for making a wide variety of sausages (*kolbassa*) with different fillings. Sausages were filled with meat (pork or beef), seasoned with spices in varying

proportions and further differentiated with the addition of pork fat, garlic or blood. They could be boiled, smoked or both. They varied greatly in size from small, thin and almost bite-sized, to big and thick, the size of a loaf of bread.

Originally, sausages were made by butchers or in the homes of people who owned cattle. Around the end of the 19th century, sausage making factories appeared. This brought standardization to the ingredients that went into each type of sausage and improved affordability (the homemade method was based on available ingredients and the sausage maker's preferences). It is around this time that recipes containing sausage, like *solyanka* (see p. 92) gained popularity.

During this period, people who rented small apartments without kitchens relied heavily on tea with open-faced sandwiches and a variety of sausages as their main staple foods. Railway stations all had a special buffet that served tea with *pirozhki*, as well as open-faced sandwiches topped with cheese or sausage. Sausages were often served as *zakuski* and used as convenient travel food or an ingredient in recipes like *solyanka*. Affordability, variety and versatility have made sausage one of Russia's favourite foods still to this day.

FISH

THE RUSSIAN TERRITORY is blessed with oceans, rivers and lakes filled with fish—from giant Lake Baikal and large rivers like the Ob River, the Volga River and the Amur River to smaller local rivers, creeks and domestic ponds. The importance of fish and fishing are clearly reflected in Russian folklore and there are a great many sayings, known to this day, that refer to fish. One example is the very popular proverb "without work you won't be able to catch any fish in the pond" (*bez truda ne vilovish i ribku iz pruda*). Fishing is used to illustrate the notion that effort is required to achieve your goal.

Fish was an important part of the Russian diet as it was readily available throughout the year and provided a valuable source of protein. It was more affordable than meat and could be used in many different dishes regardless of season. Long winter months allowed for safe transportation of fish over great distances, and meat restrictions during Lent created a strong demand for fish. Fish markets were always abundant with a rich variety of fish. Even during the tough period of time after the Russian Revolution, fish was included in rations as a mandatory staple food item along with bread and flour.

In addition to fish fillets, Russian cuisine also featured other parts of the fish—livers, heads and of course caviar (fish eggs). The most prized and renowned fish were from the *Acipenseridae* family—more commonly known as sturgeon. Once numerous and abundant, they were a frequent centerpiece on the tables; however, sturgeon became victims of chronic overfishing and now are rare and expensive. Other types of freshwater fish like burbot (*nalim*) and zander (*sudak*) were used for fish soups, *pirozhki* and larger *pirogi*. In the 19th century, a taste for trout came from Europe, and trout was farmed and served at fancy aristocratic dinners as a fashionable entree.

Fish was prepared in many different ways—dried, smoked, salted, boiled, steamed, stewed, baked and fried. Give Salmon, Rice and Egg *Koulebyaka* (see p. 140) a try; it's a great tasting traditional fish recipe. Even smaller-sized, less valuable varieties of fish were put to use. They make the best *Ukha* (see p. 88), a traditional Russian fish soup.

Dairy

TO THIS DAY, FRESH RAW COW'S MILK is highly prized in Russia for its nutritional benefits and unsurpassed taste. It is commonly believed that fresh raw milk, with its higher fat content, is superior in taste and quality to store-bought pasteurized milk. The milk available to purchase in most large cities will be pasteurized, yet many people still prefer to drink raw milk and it can be legally purchased from dairy farmers and private cow owners in villages. Goats are also kept as dairy animals and their wool is highly prized for softness and warmth, however goat meat is not usually consumed.

Russians have developed many traditional dairy products that can be made in a normal domestic set up and do not require complicated processing. Some, like *varenec* or *toplenoe moloko* (baked milk) used to be consumed as drinks but they are not so popular these days. *Ryazhenka prostokvasha* and kefir are very well-known beverages that are a great source of probiotics and are extremely refreshing. *Sivorotka* and *pakhta* are primarily used as ingredients in cooking, though *sivorotka* can also be taken as a beverage. Learn more about these and other dairy products used in Russian cuisine on the table on the next page.

DAIRY PRODUCT	DESCRIPTION
Fermented milk *Kefir*	A dairy product that is obtained from cow's milk and fermented with lactic acid and alcohol. A specific strain of kefir bacteria has to be added to trigger the process. Kefir has a thick texture, and specific sour effervescent flavour. It was specifically recommended for consumption for children and during the Soviet period it was a frequently used snack item in kindergartens and hospitals.
Butter *Maslo*	Cow's milk butter is a very popular cooking ingredient, as well as a spread for bread. Melted butter is a traditional sauce used for dipping of the Russian blini during Maslenitsa—a late-winter festival. Most of the time butter used in Russian cuisine is unsalted. *Vologodskoe maslo* is a specific type of unsalted butter from the Vologda region, invented in the 19th century. It is mainly known for its characteristic nutty flavour, obtained through a specific processing of fresh cream at high temperatures and is used for the same purposes as regular butter.
Buttermilk *Pakhta*	Cream without any fat, resulting from butter making. *Pakhta* contains good quantities of vitamins and lactic acid bacteria that are beneficial for the maintenance of good health. It is most often used in cooking.
Sour milk *Prostokvasha*	A fermented dairy product that is essentially whole regular milk that has gone sour through the fermentation process by specific strains of lactic bacteria. *Prostokvasha* is often recommended as a special dietary product that is easy to digest and is high in essential nutrients. Presence of lactic bacteria makes it a great probiotic food that helps to normalize function of the digestive tract. Due to the simplicity of its preparation it is not usually sold in stores, so most often homemade *prostokvasha* is consumed (see p. 170).
Ryazhenka	A fermented milk product obtained from baked milk that has gone through lactic acid fermentation. Specific bacterial strains are used for *ryazhenka* and it takes about 3 to 6 hours to get the end product. *Ryazhenka* has a characteristic tan to light brown colour and a specific sour taste. It is usually consumed straight as a drink.

Condensed milk *Sgushenka*	Concentrated milk, usually with sugar added, which is traditionally packaged in tin cans. It is a popular ingredient in home baking and can be used to make homemade caramel-like candy by gently heating the sweet condensed milk mass until it turns light brown. This was a treasured ingredient for many desserts.
Whey *Sivorotka*	*Sivorotka* is a byproduct of cheese processing, resulting from a coagulation of milk proteins after the addition of acidic ingredients. It can be consumed as a drink or used as an ingredient in recipes, such as pancakes.
Sour cream *Smetana*	A dairy product obtained from the upper layer of sour milk. A high fat content is highly desirable in this product. Sour cream is often used as a garnish in soups, salads and in main dishes.
Baked milk *Toplenoe moloko*	A dairy product made from whole milk by heating it at a constant low temperature for a long period of time. It has a characteristic tan colour, a thick texture and a slightly nutty taste. This product traditionally was made on the Russian stove, but with the disappearance of the traditional stove and the decrease in availability of full fat whole milk, the original recipe was lost. There are some adapted versions of baked milk, however, that are suitable for modern gas and electric stoves.
Unsalted, pressed cottage cheese *Tvorog*	A fermented dairy product rich in protein that is obtained through the curdling of milk and the removal of whey. There are several different methods of making *tvorog*, and some of them are suitable for making in modern kitchens with store-bought ingredients (see p. 166). *Tvorog* is one of the staple dairy foods in Russian cuisine and can be eaten on its own or used as an ingredient in cooking. *Tvorog* is used to make a traditional sweet Easter dish *Paskha* (see p. 158), resembling cheesecake in taste. Though *tvorog* is usually bought in stores, homemade *tvorog* is typically of much better quality.
Varenec	A fermented milk product obtained from *toplenoe moloko* (baked milk) that has gone through lactic acid fermentation. Sour cream is added to fresh baked milk and is left in a closed container in a warm place for 3 to 4 hours. In the Ural area, sour cream was occasionally substituted with fresh cream. It is one of the ancient dairy products and is consumed as a drink.

Specifics of Russian Food Preparation

OVER THE CENTURIES TYPES OF CULTIVATED FRUITS and vegetables and the cooking methods associated with them have evolved, but to this day Russian cuisine has preserved several characteristic traits that make it different from Western European or Eastern Asian cuisine. One such trait is cooking foods with the Russian oven. The specific construction and shape of this oven allows for a very specific temperature regime that can make cooking several dishes that require different cooking settings possible at the same time in one oven. This was the main influence on the formation of the traditional Russian foods.

Another typical trait of Russian cuisine is extensive use of dried and pickled vegetables and mushrooms as ingredients in dishes. Short summers and long, cold winters meant that there was a need for preservation of quickly perishable items such as tender vegetables, berries, fruits, mushrooms, meats and fish. This triggered the development of different methods for pickling, drying and freezing.

All About the Russian Oven

THERE IS NO TRADITIONAL RUSSIAN CUISINE without the key element—the Russian oven. The Russian oven was literally the heart of the home. It was a large multifunctional device that served several purposes: heating the room, cooking food and providing a warm place to sleep. There were several designs of typical Russian ovens, and they could be painted plain white or decorated with colourful ceramic tiles—*izrazci*. These tiles evolved into a unique Russian art form and came in a variety of shapes and colours with protruding ornaments or painted-on colourful miniatures showing floral motifs, scenes of people, real and mythological animals, buildings and ships. With the advancement of the industry, handmade Russian oven tiles became replaced by factory-made tiles with more consistent quality.

Due to the Russian oven's remarkable capability of heat retention over long periods of time, it kept the room warm. The usual shape of the Russian oven included a large shelf-like area—*lezhanka*—that warmed up during the day while the stove was used for cooking, and slowly released heat overnight. The smoke escape system within such an oven is usually a complex arrangement of layered brick passages that allow for maximum heat retention. In the times without central heating this mechanism of heat retention proved to be a very efficient way of maintaining a comfortable ambient temperature during the cold winter months.

Inside the oven there was a large chamber, so large that a grown man could fit inside (which was sometimes necessary for cleaning purposes to remove ashes from burnt wood deep inside the oven). Due to its size, temperature and heat intensity varied, depending on the proximity to the open flame or hot coals. This concept allowed for the simultaneous cooking of several dishes which required different cooking temperatures.

Soups, kashas and similar dishes were usually cooked in ceramic or cast iron pots, while breads, *pirogi* and other baked goods were placed directly onto hot bricks. Special tools with long handles were used to place these pots and breads into the hot oven. Cooking food in the Russian oven took significantly longer than modern stovetop cooking, so some dishes were cooked overnight, with a gradually decreasing cooking temperature. This method of cooking produced an absolutely different taste in dishes that is quite hard to reproduce now. With the complete abolition of the use of the Russian oven, some dishes were lost because it was impossible to recreate the necessary cooking environment. A good example of a lost dish is malted milk. A jar of milk was placed in the oven and kept there overnight. As a result of slow cooking with a gradual decrease in heat over time the milk acquired a thicker homogenous texture, a pleasant tan colour and a nutty rich flavour. Recreation of this exact recipe is not possible in a modern oven.

During recent years there was a revival of interest in Russian ovens, and made-to-order Russian ovens are not a rare item. However, now they are mostly used for decoration or heating purposes, rather than cooking.

Life Without a Fridge

SHORT SUMMERS AND LONG, COLD WINTERS created a natural need for preservation of harvests. Russian people were very creative with their methods of food preservation. Up until the invention of the refrigerator perishable food was stored in root cellars, often located outside the house, with an entrance at ground level somewhere in the yard. Root cellars were used to keep potatoes, beets, onions, carrots, beverages and all sorts of pickles. This was called a *lednik*, and was a special underground or above ground construction, filled during winter with ice blocks. Insulation in a *lednik* was so good that ice could last throughout the whole summer until the next snowfall. Most perishable items such as milk, dairy and fresh produce was stored in there.

The Russian Oven by Evdokia Obukhova,
2014. PRIVATE COLLECTION.

The Russian oven was the heart of the house. All life of this peasant house is rotating around the oven—day and night. Behind the blue curtain you can see the patchwork blanket—this is the sleeping place that is warmed by the heat given off by the oven. On the bench under the oven you can see a pair of Russian birch bark shoes—*lapti*—a typical peasant shoe. Next to the *lapti* there are three items: the samovar, a wooden tray used for cabbage cutting and a clay jug for milk or water. Close to the opening of the oven, where all the cooking action takes place, you can see tools used for placing items inside the oven: the *ukhvat*—the wrought metal horn-shaped pot holder on a long handle (there are two of them in this painting) and the *lopata*—a big wooden bread shovel used to place bread and *pirogi* inside the oven. There is a cast iron pot (*gorshok*—a larger version of the ceramic *gorshochki*, used in our Beet and Sour Cream Pots recipe on p. 109) inside the oven, most likely filled with kasha or *schi*.

Food Preservation

There were several main food preservation methods that are still used to this day:

PRESERVATION METHOD	DESCRIPTION
Fermentation *Kvashenie*	A process of fermenting vegetables with the aid of lactic acid–producing bacteria naturally present on the surface of the vegetables. Most often it was used for cabbage, cucumbers and tomatoes. Pickling is the process of preserving food in an acidic solution, such as vinegar; fermentation of food is the process of preserving food with help of lactic acid bacteria or yeast that convert naturally present sugars in the food into acids, carbon dioxide gas and/or alcohol, depending on the method of fermentation. In Russian cuisine, fermentation is used to preserve vegetables such as cabbage, cucumbers and tomatoes through the addition of salt brine to the vegetables creating the conditions necessary for the development of the lactic acid bacteria that drives the fermentation process. This process was (and still is) one of the most popular ways of preserving vegetables for the winter. Pickled foods are an important component of *zakuski* (appetizers).
Soaking *Mochenie*	A method for the preservation of fragile fruits and berries. In some cases, with apples for example, *mochenie* involves fermentation, which results in a change in the flavour and texture of the fruit. For long-term storage, berries were typically soaked in water. Berries containing bacterial growth–inhibiting benzoic acid, such as cranberries and lingonberries, could be preserved in plain water indefinitely without risk of fermentation. Berries gave a pink colour and a subtle flavour to the liquid in which they were preserved. This liquid was often used as a refreshing drink. The soaking solution for apples consisted of a mixture of sugar, honey, salt, mustard, rye flour and some aromatic herbs. Most often this method of preservation was used for apples and pears. Soaked apples were served as *zakuski* together with other preserves such as Russian sauerkraut and dill pickles.

Drying *Sushenie*	A traditional method of preserving mushrooms. Dried mushrooms have an extensive shelf life and a much stronger flavour than raw mushrooms. Berries and some fruits were also dried. Dried mushrooms were typically used in soups, rehydrated for pastry filling and present as key ingredients in Lent dishes. In preparation for drying, mushrooms were strung spaced apart on a thread hung horizontally along the kitchen ceiling. Once completely dry they were either stored hung up on a wall on the string or placed in a dry jar.
Sweet preserves *Varenye*	A Russian jam in which intact berries or fruit pieces were preserved in transparent sugar or honey syrup. Another similar type of preservation involved soaking entire fruits in honey. Any fruits or berries could be used to make *varenye*. Preparation of *varenye* involved a long process of heating and cooling the fruit or berries in heavy syrup in order to allow the fruit to be completely soaked with syrup and to retain its original shape (see p. 159–160).
Freezing *Zamorozka*	Fish and meats were sold frozen solid during the winter months. This ensured the safety of the food and allowed more time to sell the catch of the day. In order to prepare fish or meat for long-term storage it was cleaned (gutted, cut in pieces, etc.) and left out in the cold to freeze. Once completely frozen, fish or meat could be transported or placed into a *lednik* for storage.

TRADITIONAL RUSSIAN TEA

I F YOU EVER VISIT RUSSIA or happen to be invited into a Russian home anywhere in the world, chances are you will be offered tea. It is possibly the most prevalent Russian tradition that is still alive today. Tea drinking is a very important part of Russian culture. No matter what the occasion, even if there is no occasion, there is always time and space for tea. It is most often black tea and it is served in a very particular manner.

Over the centuries a specific Russian tea ceremony had developed, which is observed to this day with very minor adjustments. The Russian tea ceremony is probably not so well known, and definitely not as formal as the Japanese tea ceremony, or the British five-o'clock cup of tea with milk and sugar; however, it has distinct features which make it quite different from any other food intake during the day.

Tea came to Russia in the early 17th century and over the years gained popularity until Russia became the largest tea-drinking country in the world. In the 17th century Russia had special trade agreements with China, from which it imported good-quality tea directly.

The Samovar

Before electricity became common in Russia, the centerpiece of the Russian tea ceremony was the samovar. Perhaps you have seen images of a large fancy metal vessel with a little tap on the side, perched somewhere on the table. The samovar is often placed next to other stereotypical Russian items, such as the *balalaika* (a musical instrument), *shapka oushanka* (a winter hat), dancing bears and caviar. But not everyone knows how the samovar worked.

The direct translation of the word samovar is "auto-boil" or "self-boil." This is the essence of its function—it is a self contained, portable boiling system for heating water.

ORIGINS

The exact date of samovar invention is unknown, but it most likely appeared shortly after the introduction of tea to the Russian market in the 17th century. In the early 19th century, Nikita Demidov, a merchant from Tula, visited the Ural mountain region with skilled workers from his factories, who specialized in working with copper and other blacksmithing crafts. It is possible that during this business visit a prototype of the samovar, used earlier in that particular region, was noticed and designated for mass production by the Tula factories and artisans.

DESIGN

Over the years the design of the samovar has slightly changed, but the manufacturing process remains the same. Samovar shapes were influenced by fashion and by the end of 19th century Tula produced as many as 150 different styles of samovar. With the development of mass industry and Demidov's ambition to produce large quantities of affordable samovars, designs of the samovars were simplified. Two of the most popular designs were "jar" and "stem glass," which referred to their overall shapes. "Jar" shaped samovars had a cylindrical water reservoir, and "stem glass" shaped samovars had a reservoir resembling a wine glass, narrow at the bottom and wider at the top. Tula also produced travel samovars for voyages. They would be smaller in size than the regular tabletop samovars, were less ornate and often had a metal teapot included to make a set.

The city of Tula is the most famous samovar-making region in Russia. The 19th century saw the peak of the samovar's popularity with the development of industrial factories and the possibility of mass producing consumer goods, and the samovar became a common item in all households from the nobility to the peasantry, from the Baltic Sea to Kamchatka.

CONSTRUCTION

Construction of the samovar is more complex than it seems from the outside and it takes certain skills to properly boil the water in it.

Samovars are usually made of brass, however other alloys can be used and silver and gold can be used for plating.

Along the centre axis of the samovar runs a vertical fuel shaft. This is where coal, wood chips or pine cones are loaded and burned. These materials do not give off unpleasant aromas while burning and are small enough to fit inside the fuel shaft, which narrows closer to the top of the reservoir. Gases are allowed to escape via the same shaft going upwards past the water reservoir, which surrounds the fuel shaft completely. This allows for the maximum heat exchange between the burning fuel and the water in the reservoir. The heat distribution from the burning fuel is different throughout the shaft—hotter at the bottom, closer to the fire, and slightly cooler at the top where only hot gases, the product of burning fuel, are escaping. This heat distribution is essential for fast and efficient heating of the water in the reservoir.

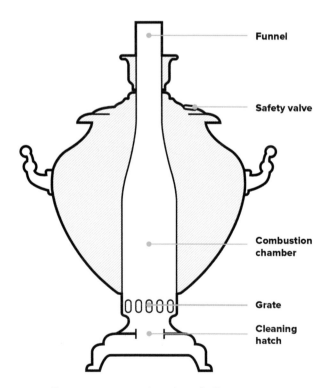

Samovar cross section. Anatoly Gromov, 2014

Under the fuel shaft, a grid allows air to access the burning fuel inside the samovar. Without oxygen there is no burning process, so adequate ventilation is vital.

A detachable tube creates an air current, moving the fresh air from the bottom of the air shaft up through the grid, feeding the fire and carrying out gases. The tube is placed in the top of the samovar's air shaft. Sometimes this detachable tube was directly connected to the smoke-escape system of the home wood furnace, creating an even stronger air current.

USING THE SAMOVAR

To use the samovar, several large coal pieces are placed at the bottom of the fuel shaft, on the grid, and the reservoir is filled with water. Then a couple of wooden chips are ignited and lowered into the fuel shaft. This should be sufficient to start the fire. Once the fire is started, more fuel can be added and the tube extension can be placed on top of the shaft to create the air flow. Heat from the bottom part of the fuel shaft, where the coals are burning, is transferred to the water at the bottom of the reservoir. The hot water from the bottom rises to the top, pushing the cooler water from the top of the reservoir closer to the bottom where it is then heated. This movement creates natural convection. The water is evenly mixed through and the heating is equal throughout the whole reservoir. This is an extremely energy efficient method of boiling water.

When the samovar starts to make noise, it is a clear indication that the water will boil within 2 to 3 minutes. This noise is called "samovar singing." The detachable tube is necessary only during the burning of the fuel. Once the water has boiled, the tube is removed and an empty porcelain teapot is placed on top of the fuel shaft. This heats up the porcelain pot for optimal tea brewing, and stalls the airflow within the fuel shaft to extinguish the fire. Then the samovar can be safely placed on a metal tray and moved from the kitchen to the tea table. In order to set a table for a traditional Russian tea, such as those that happened at the end of the 19th century, you will need to have on hand at least some of the items in the chart on pages 54 and 55.

Merchant Wife at Tea Table by Boris Kustodiev, 1918. ©2014, STATE RUSSIAN MUSEUM, ST. PETERSBOURG.

This image depicts a merchant's wife at the tea table. Note the traditional pear-shaped samovar on the table; porcelain cups and saucers; fresh fruit, including a juicy watermelon; and a little basket with baked goods—raisin loaf, some buns and cookies. Note the crystal *vazochka* with cherry *varenye* hiding behind the watermelon.

Traditional Table Settings

TABLE SETTING ITEM	DESCRIPTION
Samovar	A large metal vessel that boils water and keeps it hot.
Metal trays *Zhestyanie podnosi*	Flat trays on which the samovar and other hot items are placed, to keep the tablecloth clean and keep the hot items from direct contact with the table. Trays were widely used and evolved into an art form, covered with intricate decorations. The most well known are the trays from the Zhostovo region.
Teapot *Zavarochnyi chainik*	Usually porcelain, Russian teapots are small in order to fit on top of the samovar. Sometimes metal teapots were used when travelling, but they were otherwise used very rarely as metal affects the flavour of the brewing tea. Porcelain was always the preferred material for teapots and their small size allowed for the preparation of a concentrated tea called *zavarka* that was later diluted in each cup with hot water according to taste.
Tea strainer *Sitechko*	A silver tool used to strain the tea leaves when pouring tea. Since loose-leaf black tea was always used for brewing, this was an essential tool used to keep floating leaves away from the cup. Some porcelain pots have built-in strainers, but often an additional, finer strainer is used to make sure no debris ends up in the cup.
Tea container *Zavarochnica*	The porcelain or metal container in which tea leaves are stored to ensure their freshness and quality.
Sugar bowl *Saharnica*	A small round bowl, usually made of porcelain, with two handles and a lid. The sugar served is usually solid sugar that has been broken into bite-sized pieces, or crystalline beet sugar (called "sand sugar").
Sugar tongs or sugar spoon *Shipci dlya sahara*	Usually silver and used to take sugar from the sugar bowl. (It is not acceptable to touch sugar with your hand!)

Saucers *Bludca*	Small saucers, usually rosette-shaped and made of porcelain or glass, are used to serve individual portions of *varenye* (Russian jam). Larger saucers go under cups and can also be used for baked goods.
Glass or crystal stemmed bowl *Vazochka dlya varenya*	A bowl on a stem and with a lid, usually made of glass or crystal, is used to serve *varenye*. *Varenye* is transferred from the glass jar where it is kept into the delicate crystal bowl of the *vazochka* and is covered with a lid and then served that way at the tea table.
Basket *Korzinka*	Baskets woven from thin strips of wood, birch bark or thin branches are used to serve traditional baked goods. Typically they do not have a handle, so it is easier to grab the contents.
Creamer *Molochnik*	A small vessel, usually porcelain, used to serve cream for the tea.
Tea towel *Polotence*	Russian tea towels are usually made from local linen.
Napkins *Salfetki*	Napkins, one per each person, are usually made from linen. They are placed under the teacup on the table during tea drinking.
Teacups *Chainie chashki*	In the late 19th century there were two distinct types of cups used to drink tea. Light glasses set in metal holders allowed for maintaining the optimal tea temperature, along with visibility of the colour of the tea (especially important for tea drinking in public places to ensure that the tea was strong enough and dark enough) and a cool grip. These glasses in metal holders are seldom used at home but are traditionally used to this day on trains in Russia. The other type were porcelain cups in a classic table setting, which were always set on a saucer.

Baked Goods

One characteristic trait of Russian tea drinking is consumption of a variety of baked goods and other snacks. Some of the baked goods you would serve during a traditional Russian tea would be:

BAKED GOOD	DESCRIPTION
Kalach	A Moscow-region invention that looks pretty much like a bun with a round handle on the side (see p. 134). It was invented as street food, so you could hold it by the handle, eat the bun and then discard the part that you touched with unwashed hands.
Baranki/sushki	Small dry rings of dough with a shiny dry glaze. In the past they were sold strung on a string, now they are available in plastic bags. They are usually broken into four parts by hand and then eaten. They have a slightly sweet flavour. These items were always bought at bakeries.
Gingerbread *Pryaniki*	A sweet, heavy spice bread, such as gingerbread, that is a very popular treat for kids (see p. 152). *Pryaniki* are sugar glazed and sometimes have fillings. *Pryaniki* come in a variety of shapes and sizes and different flavours. Press boards for *pryaniki* have intricate images of animals, plants, people and messages carved on wood. They are a special art form and many of them can be found in Russian museums. The dough was pressed into the carved board before baking in order to get a decorative image on the surface of the *pryanik*.
Cookies *Pechenye*	A variety of home-baked cookies were made especially for tea. They were never used as a snack food or dessert. Only as an accompaniment to tea. See Soviet Era Recipes.
Sweet pirozhki *Sladkie pirozhki*	Yeast dough baked dumplings with a sweet filling of thick jam, almost always homemade. You can find *pirozhki* recipes in Traditional Old Recipes.
Pastries, cakes *Pirogi, torti*	These can be homemade or store bought, and not necessarily eaten just for special occasions. See Soviet Era Recipes.
Candy *Konfeti*	All sorts of chocolate, caramel, sugar and other candies are always a welcome accompaniment to tea. See Traditional Old Recipes.

Sometimes savoury snacks are also served with tea (especially if it replaces a light meal such as breakfast or if the hostess decides to make tea drinking into a more substantial meal). Typical accompaniment for tea at such occasions would be open-faced sandwiches. Tea with sandwiches remains a typical full meal replacement for students and people who for various reasons cannot afford to have a complete cooked meal at home. During the Soviet period, tea with open-faced sandwiches and sweets was a common treat for guests.

Once everything is set on the table and the water in the samovar is boiling, it is time to brew the tea. In order to do that you should take the warm porcelain teapot from the top of the samovar, place the dry tea leaves (loose leaf black tea is most often used by the Russians) inside at the proportion of one teaspoon per person and one teaspoon for the pot. Half-fill the tea pot with hot water from the samovar and place it back on top of the samovar.

After three to five minutes the pot can be filled to the top. This creates a relatively small amount of very strong-brewed tea. Unlike in Britain, this tea does not fill the cup, but rather it is used as a concentrate, which is then diluted by hot water directly from the samovar. This way everyone at the table can have the strength of tea in their cup adjusted to their liking, but have the same strength of brewed tea from the teapot.

In a way Russian tea drinking can be considered a light meal, but unlike breakfast, lunch or dinner it does not have a traditional fixed time of the day when it is taken. Russian tea drinking can take place absolutely any time of the day and anywhere—at home, at a restaurant, on the road while travelling and most importantly when guests arrive. It is absolutely necessary to set up tea drinking when guests come, even if you just had your own tea half an hour ago. It can be as simple as just tea with *varenye* and some cookies from the closest bakery or as complex as the list of all of the above items set up for the guests. Because of the flexibility of when it can happen and the availability of all the necessary items for the tea drinking, the quantity of tea consumed per day by Russians is unsurpassed.

Giving Tea Different Flavours

SOME OF THE ITEMS AT THE TABLE you can add directly into the tea. The tea acquires a new flavour and can taste completely different from regular black tea, depending on what is added.

One of the items most often added is *varenye* (Russian jam). *Varenye* is added to the tea when it is already in the cup; the fruits sink to the bottom and the syrup gives the tea a distinct flavour and colour. Russian *varenye* has a different texture, compared to typical North American or British jam. High quality *varenye* is supposed to have intact berries or fruit pieces in translucent thick syrup. The addition of North American jam to tea will give a completely different result because North American jam contains too much pectin to be dissolved completely. Also, many Western jams do not usually contain any intact fruit or berries, which help to create a visually appealing drink. You can find *varenye* recipes on pages 159 and 160.

Other popular additions to tea include cream, lemon, mint, linden flowers, rum, cognac and Madeira. It is interesting to note that fresh lemons were always a common sight in Russia, and primarily they were not store-bought but homegrown. Over the years Russians have developed several lemon cultivars that grow very well on window sills. These small compact bushes are able to bloom and bear fruit regardless of what the weather is like outside.

Modern Russian Tea Drinking

MODERN TEA DRINKING IS STILL essentially the same as it was back in the 19th century, with minor adjustments—the samovar has been replaced by electrical or stovetop tea kettles, glasses with metal holders are quite rare nowadays and new kinds of tea such as tea in bags and flavoured tea is now available.

Everything else remains the same, but what is most important is that people's enjoyment also remains the same—in the 19th century a merchant from Moscow could enjoy his tea drinking with friends and family on a warm summer evening the same way that tea is now enjoyed by modern Russians sitting comfortably around a small apartment's kitchen table. The only thing that is missing is the iconic samovar—the symbol of the Russian tea drinking ceremony.

TRADITIONAL OLD RECIPES

RADITIONAL RUSSIAN CUISINE formed gradually and it took the effort of many local and foreign chefs to refine and organize authentic recipes. This was a formidable task as recipes were typically passed along from one cook to another, from old to young, and very seldom were they written down. Usually such "recipes" were in the form of personal notes with few, if any, measurements and only brief instructions. It wasn't until the publication of books such as A *Gift to Young Housewives* by Elena Molokhovets and *Practical Basics of Culinary Art* by Pelageya Alexandrova-Ignatieva that recipes were formalized and became popular references for average households.

In this chapter you will find a collection of older Russian home recipes. It will focus on homemade dishes that could be found in the majority of Russian households regardless of their social class and wealth. Ancient dishes like kasha, *schi* and *kvas* were cooked and enjoyed in Russia for many centuries while other recipes like Pozharsky Cutlets (see p. 104) and Gourievskaya Kasha (see p. 149) were developed relatively recently—at the end of the 19th century. This chapter will take you from *zakuski* (appetizer) recipes to soups, main dishes, kashas, blinis and *pirogi* (baked goods) and finally desserts and beverages. By preparing one or two recipes from each section you will be able to construct a full Russian meal, complete with appetizers and beverages.

Setting the Mood

TO SET THE MOOD you will need to bring out the fancy china and a nice ornate table-cloth. Dress yourself up too, and invite a few of your dear friends (or a lot—whatever you prefer) for dinner. A pleasant conversation is the centerpiece of any Russian feast.

These suggestions are included to help you recreate the authentic feeling of old Russia.

A FILM TO WATCH: *War and Peace* directed by Sergei Bondarchuk. This movie, based on the famous epic novel by Leo Tolstoy won an Oscar for best foreign language movie. It took many years to film, and the beautiful costumes and brilliant acting make this an unforgettable movie.

MUSIC TO LISTEN TO: Tchaikovsky or a collection of Russian romance (performed by Zhanna Bichevskaya, Alexander Vertinsky, Feodor Chaliapine, Anastasia Vyaltseva) or folk songs performed by the Kuban Cossack Chorus.

A BOOK TO READ: For further reference, Nikolai Gogol's *Dead Souls* is one of the major works of 19th century Russian literature. Gogol creates unforgettable images of typical middle-class people of that era. His work is laced with delectable descriptions of all sorts of food fare—a definite must-read from a culinary perspective.

On the Terrace by Boris Kustodiev, 1906. STATE ART MUSEUM, NIZHNY NOVGOROD.

This painting depicts a typical family scene of old Russia. On a summer evening, the entire family gathered in the terrace to drink tea. You can see the jar shaped samovar in the middle of the table, some fresh fruit in the bowl and cookies. The lady in the background is drinking her tea while the mother observes the little girl.

Appetizers
Zakuski

ALTHOUGH *ZAKUSKI* ARE CURRENTLY a major and distinctive part of Russian cuisine, they only entered the scene in the late 18th century. They were largely defined in the early 19th century when French chefs were invited to work in the kitchens of prominent Russian aristocratic families. These chefs started a massive overhaul of Russian cuisine, bringing system and order to the way food was prepared and cooked. They shaped the concept of *zakuski* as a wide array of appetizers, which included very typical Russian traditional food items: pickled foods, such as mushrooms, cucumbers and tomatoes; meat either boiled or fried, but served cold; smoked meats and cold cuts; cheeses; and fish, such as herring and assorted freshwater fish. Along with simple marinades, pickles and cold cuts, more complex dishes were served.

Zakuski were served on a special separate table, and each on an individual platter beautifully arranged and lavishly garnished. It is the wide variety and dazzling assortment of *zakuski* that made it stand out as a very special part of the meal. Traditional *zakuski* are accompanied by small shots of vodka and together are meant to open up the appetite, similar in concept to the French aperitif. *Zakuski* served before lunch were typically served with several different types of vodka: vodka without sugar added such as *erofeitch* (also known as bitter vodkas) and ratafias.

Stuffed Eggs with Red Salmon Caviar

Yayca farshorovannie krasnoj ikroj

———— ❧❧ ————

7 hard-boiled eggs, peeled

2 Tbsp (30 mL) sour cream (30% fat, or the highest fat sour cream you can find)

2 Tbsp (30 mL) green onions or chives, finely chopped

1 tsp (5 mL) lemon juice

¼ tsp (1 mL) salt

½ tsp (2 mL) black pepper

¼ cup (60 mL) salmon caviar

3 lettuce leaves

4 sprigs of fresh dill or parsley

This appetizer uses salmon caviar—a very popular item in Russian cuisine.

Cut eggs in half lengthwise. Carefully remove the yolks and place them in a bowl. Reserve the egg white halves. Blend together egg yolks, sour cream, green onions, lemon juice, salt and pepper until smooth. Stuff the egg whites with this mixture and spoon a bit of the caviar on top of each. Serve chilled on a platter lined with lettuce leaves, and decorate with sprigs of fresh dill or parsley.

MAKES 14 EGG HALVES
PREPARATION TIME: 20 MINUTES

CAVIAR

There are several types of caviar that are used in Russian cuisine.

RED CAVIAR: Comes from salmon and looks like intact bright orange translucent balls, just a bit smaller in size than green peas. It is used as a garnish in many dishes, served as an appetizer or spread on top of butter on a slice of white bread.

BLACK CAVIAR: Comes from sturgeon. It is much smaller in size than red caviar and is grayish-black in colour. It is used the same way as the red caviar.

Most often caviar is store bought and is good up until the date indicated on the jar. Caviar can also be frozen.

Eggplant Caviar

Baklazhannaya ikra

1 large eggplant, whole

1 tsp (5 mL) salt (approx.)

3 Tbsp (45 mL) olive oil, divided

2 medium onions, diced

1 large tomato, diced

2 tsp (10 mL) lemon juice

salt and pepper, to taste

1 sprig of fresh parsley

1 lemon slice

This delightful and flavourful appetizer can be served by itself or as a delicious spread over rye bread. It is also known as "poor man's caviar."

Cut off the stem, peel and chop the eggplant, then sprinkle with salt to taste. Let sit at room temperature for about an hour to remove bitterness.

Pat the eggplant dry with a paper towel, but do not wipe off the salt. Heat 2 Tbsp (30 mL) olive oil in a large skillet and add the eggplant, diced onions and tomato and cook over low heat until the vegetables are tender, about 20 minutes. Add the remaining 1 Tbsp (15 mL) oil, lemon juice, salt and pepper to taste. Continue to cook over low heat, for 10 to 15 minutes. Remove the caviar from heat, cool down and serve at room temperature or chilled. Garnish with parsley and a slice of lemon.

MAKES 6 SERVINGS

PREPARATION TIME: 1 HOUR

COOKING TIME: 30 MINUTES

Pickled Chanterelle Mushrooms

Zakuska iz solenih lisičhek

2 cups (500 mL) pickled chanterelle
  mushrooms (see below)
1 large shallot, thinly sliced
2 Tbsp (30 mL) fresh dill, chopped
1 Tbsp (15 mL) fresh green onions,
  chopped
½ tsp (2 mL) black pepper
2 Tbsp (30 mL) sunflower oil

The contrast between the bright orange chanterelles and the green onions makes a very festive looking appetizer.

Slice larger chanterelles into quarters, leave small ones whole, and place in a small serving dish. Add sliced shallot, dill, green onions and freshly ground black pepper. Dress with sunflower oil and mix well. Serve on its own, chilled.

MAKES 6 SERVINGS
PREPARATION TIME: 10 MINUTES

CHANTERELLE MUSHROOMS

In Russia, chanterelles grow in every forest. In North America, canned chanterelles can usually be found in stores located in neighborhoods with a large European immigrant population. Russian, Polish and German stores are likely to have them.

Dill Pickles in Brine

Solenye ogurci

4 lb (1.8 kg) pickling cucumbers

3 cloves of garlic

1 large stalk of fresh dill with seeds

½ cup (125 mL) horseradish root, thinly sliced

2 fresh horseradish leaves

1 blackcurrant leaf (optional)

¼ cup (60 mL) salt per each 1 quart (1 L) water

BLACKCURRANT LEAVES

Pick the leaves directly from the blackcurrant bush for the most flavour. Blackcurrant leaves are difficult to find in stores. You will likely need to find a bush either in your yard, in the wild or at a blackcurrant farm.

Dill pickles are a cornerstone food in Russian cuisine. Not only are they used as a *zakuska*, but also as an important ingredient in many traditional Russian recipes, such as *rassolnik* (see p. 91) and Salad Olivier (see p. 181). Homemade dill pickles are always preferred to store-bought ones. Traditional Russian dill pickles are brined in salt; vinegar is never used in this recipe, however you may come across dill pickle recipes from other countries that use vinegar.

Use a clean 2-quart (1.9 L) glass jar with a lid. Place the cucumbers inside and add garlic, dill, horseradish root and leaves (and the black-currant leaf, if using). Fill the jar with water so that all the cucumbers are completely covered. Pour out the water, measuring its volume with a measuring cup, before placing into a saucepan. (The amount of water will vary depending on the size of the jar and the size of the cucumbers.) Bring the water that was measured out to a boil and add salt based on the amount of water (¼ cup oz [60 mL] for each 4 cups [1 L]). Once all salt is dissolved, remove from heat and pour the brine over the cucumbers; let them stand at room temperature for 2 days and then cover with a lid and keep in the refrigerator, making sure that the cucumbers are submerged in brine at all times. Pickles can be refrigerated in brine for up to 3 months.

MAKES 10 DILL PICKLES

PREPARATION TIME: 1½ HOURS + 2 DAYS FOR PICKLING

NOTE: Dill pickles can be canned to last longer than 3 months. Follow the usual canning procedures using sterilized jars and store pickles in a cool place such as a basement or cold storage room.

NOTE: Dill pickles are a great accompaniment for Pan-Fried Potatoes with Onions (see p. 216).

Clockwise from top: Russian
Sauerkraut (p. 77), Dill Pickles in
Brine (p. 73), Stuffed Eggs with
Red Salmon Caviar (p. 68), Salted
Black Radish *Zakuska* (p. 75), Green
Onions with Sour Cream (p. 75)

Green Onions with Sour Cream

Zeleniy luk so smetanoi

5 green onions, finely chopped
½ cup (125 mL) sour cream (30%)
½ tsp (2 mL) salt

This makes a nice spread over thin slices of toast. You can add some fresh dill for extra flavour.

Combine the green onions, sour cream and salt, mixing well. Serve mixture on its own in a small dish, or as a filling for hard-boiled eggs.

MAKES 4 SERVINGS
PREPARATION TIME: 5 MINUTES

Salted Black Radish *Zakuska*

Zakuska iz redki

1 large black radish (see below)
1 green onion, chopped
½ tsp (2 mL) salt
1 Tbsp (15 mL) sunflower oil
4 sprigs of fresh dill or parsley

One of the oldest recipes in this book, radishes and onions were abundant in any Russian house at any time. Black radish, along with cucumbers and herring, made the basis for appetizers eaten as an accompaniment to vodka.

Clean and peel the radish and soak in cold water for about 20 minutes. Drain the water, slice the radish thinly, and garnish with green onion. Season with salt and sunflower oil. Serve chilled.

MAKES 5 SERVINGS
PREPARATION TIME: 5 MINUTES

BLACK RADISHES

Black radishes are larger than the regular red radishes, with rough black skin and crisp white flesh. They're about the size of a medium beet and have a strong pungent flavour, similar to daikon radishes. Black radishes are one of the most typical Russian vegetables. You can find them in many farmers' markets or grow them yourself in your backyard using seeds (most seed merchants would have them).

Pickled Gruzdi Mushrooms

Gruzdi solenye

2 lb (1 kg) raw gruzdi mushrooms (see below)

1 handful + 3 Tbsp (45 mL) pickling salt

2 horseradish leaves

4 blackcurrant leaves (see p. 73)

4 cloves garlic, coarsely chopped

7 whole black peppercorns

1 bunch of dill with flowers

GRUZDI MUSHROOMS

Gruzdi mushrooms (*Lactarius resimus*) have a dense white flesh and dark gray skin. They have a delicate, slightly nutty flavour and a wonderful fresh mushroom aroma. When pickled they become crispy like cucumber pickles. Their attractive shape—smooth and round with a little dent in the middle of the cap—and texture makes them a very visually appealing *zakuska*. Presoaking gruzdi mushrooms before pickling is necessary to remove bitter white juice from the mushrooms.

Typically, Russians pick wild mushrooms in the forest, then pickle or dry them for the winter months. Gruzdi mushrooms are unfortunately difficult to find in North America.

Thoroughly clean and wash the mushrooms. Cut the larger ones in half and leave smaller ones whole. Place the mushrooms in a large enamel-coated or glass pan; add a handful of salt and cover with cold water. Drain the water after 4 hours. Add more cold water. Let the mushrooms soak 2 to 3 days, changing the water 3 times per day without adding extra salt to remove any bitter flavours from the mushrooms.

Line the bottom of a large pickling jar (about 14 cups [3.5 L] volume) with horseradish leaves, then in layers add mushrooms with caps facing down, 3 Tbsp (45 mL) salt, blackcurrant leaves, garlic, black peppercorns and dill. Cover the top mushroom layer with a clean cheesecloth and press down with a clean solid round object (such as a ceramic saucer or wooden disc). Place a weight on top to keep the mushrooms submerged under brine. Cover the top with another layer of clean cheesecloth and let stand at a cool ambient temperature, such as in a basement or cold storage room. Mushrooms will be thoroughly pickled in about 3 weeks. At this time, they can be placed in sterilized jars and canned for future use.

MAKES 10 SERVINGS
PREPARATION TIME: 2 TO 3 DAYS PRE-SOAKING +30 MINUTES ASSEMBLY + 3 WEEKS PICKLING

Russian Sauerkraut

Kvashenaya kapusta

2 lb (1 kg) head of white
   cabbage, shredded

1 large carrot, grated

1½ Tbsp (22 mL) pickling or
   kosher salt

NOTE: Do not use table salt
as it will make the sauerkraut
bitter, and do not add water, as
the end product will be limp.

NOTE: For a little variety, add
1 medium beet (julienned) or
½ cup (125 mL) fresh cranberries to the basic sauerkraut recipe. If using a beet,
mix it together well with the
cabbage and salt (the carrot may be omitted). If using
cranberries, first mix together
cabbage, salt and carrot, and
then add the cranberries. The
beet gives the sauerkraut a
lovely pink colour, and the
cranberry adds an attractive
and flavourful finish.

Sauerkraut is another staple in Russian cuisine. Made by fermenting in salt brine without vinegar, Russian sauerkraut can be eaten
on its own, as an appetizer, or used as an ingredient in many other
dishes. This method of preparation should be used for all recipes in
this book that call for sauerkraut as an ingredient.

In a large, deep enamel or glass dish, mix cabbage, carrot and salt vigorously by hand, making sure cabbage is well bruised and starts giving juice. Taste the cabbage for salt; at minimum it should taste saltier
than you'd like it in a salad. Not enough salt will leave the cabbage dry.
Press the cabbage down with a spoon, place a dinner plate on top of it
and add a solid weight (a clean well-sealed, heavy water bottle will do).
Make sure the cabbage is completely immersed in its own juice.

Store at room temperature for 2 days to start the fermentation process. During this period, if you see any foam appearing on the surface,
remove it with a spoon. Each day, mix the cabbage well to let the gas
bubbles escape, then replace the weight and submerge the cabbage in
its juice.

After 2 days, remove the weight and the plate, transfer the sauerkraut into a glass jar with a tight lid and move the cabbage to a cool
environment such as the bottom of the refrigerator or a cool basement.
At this time, most of the brine should be absorbed and the sauerkraut
is ready to be eaten.

MAKES 20 SERVINGS

PREPARATION TIME: 1 HOUR + 2 DAYS FOR PICKLING

Sauerkraut as *Zakuska*

1 cup (250 mL) sauerkraut

1 shallot, finely sliced

2 Tbsp (30 mL) sunflower oil

1 tsp (5 mL) sugar

1 sprig of fresh parsley

Place 1 cup (250 mL) sauerkraut into a serving bowl, add sliced shallot, sunflower oil and sugar. Mix well and garnish with parsley. Serve
chilled.

MAKES 4 SERVINGS

PREPARATION TIME: 15 MINUTES

MY MOTHER'S MEMOIR: *Winter Market*

Moscow's winter market is abundant with all sorts of pickles and salted preserves. White marble tables proudly display heaps of sauerkraut, dill pickles, soaked apples and salted garlic sprouts. Every vendor has his or her own heirloom recipe for sauerkraut or pickles that they bring to the market, and all of them are different. One sauerkraut is best for schi, another goes better with roasted meat, and one mixed with cranberries is best served as zakuska. It's impossible to just pass by without tasting them all. A little bite here, a tiny bite there, offered by generous vendors, in an attempt to persuade you that their sauerkraut is absolutely the best. And they are all correct.

SAUERKRAUT STORAGE

Sauerkraut is best when it is prepared in large batches. It can be stored at a constant temperature of 32°F to 37°F (0°C to 3°C). A cold basement, garage or cold storage room are great places for sauerkraut storage.

A large batch of sauerkraut can be kept in the same dish where it was fermented. It is very important to make sure the top surface is not exposed to air, which may cause spoilage. No refrigeration is required in this case. After removing portions, make sure the sauerkraut is properly covered and weighted down. A small amount of spoilage may appear after each opening, but it can be safely removed just before taking out the next portion needed. This method of storage can keep sauerkraut in good condition through the whole winter.

Sauerkraut can also be stored in tightly sealed jars in the refrigerator. Jars don't have to be sterilized if you are keeping them in the refrigerator and this method of storage is good for small batches of sauerkraut that will be used up within 2 to 3 months

Soups

USSIAN SOUP IS A STAPLE usually served with kasha and bread. It was traditionally prepared in special-shaped clay or cast iron pots with narrow bottoms and wide openings in the Russian oven. Traditional soup preparation required many hours, but the resulting flavour was dramatically different from the soups prepared on electric or gas stove tops. Russian soup is heavily influenced by the seasonality of the ingredients. Some soups are considered spring dishes and contain fresh greens typical of the season. Summer soups tend to contain more fresh vegetables such as young carrots, marrow squash and fresh tomatoes. Spring and summer soups are usually light and refreshing dishes; fall and winter soups tend to be richer with a heavier consistency.

Traditional Russian soups can be divided into several major categories:

KIND OF SOUP	DESCRIPTION
Schi	Vegetable soup made with fresh cabbage or Russian sauerkraut as the main ingredient.
Ukha	Fish soup that is very popular due to the abundance of freshwater fish throughout Russia (saltwater fish is also used) and the large number of Lent days, when fish was allowed but meat was forbidden. Sometimes broth from *ukha* is used as a sauce or a side dish for other dishes.
Solyanka	A complex thick soup in which the broth and the solid ingredients are cooked separately and then combined. Characterized by a salty and sour taste and by the use of pickled or fermented ingredients, such as pickled cucumbers.
Borscht	A traditional Ukrainian soup made with beets which gained popularity in Russia and is now considered as common as *schi*.
Noodle soup	This type of soup most likely came to Russia with the Tatar invasion and was adapted to local tastes. Noodles made from wheat dough are accompanied by a light meat, vegetable or mushroom broth. Other ingredients such as root vegetables or herbs can be added as well.
Rassolnik	A specific type of soup that uses Russian pickled cucumbers. The Russian style of pickling differs from American in a particular way—vinegar is never used, only strong salt brine.
Pokhlebka	A variety of clear soup usually made without meat broth as a base. Onions, fresh herbs and grains such as barley are typical ingredients in *pokhlebka*.
Botvinia	*Botvinia* is a cold soup that has three components which were traditionally served on separate plates and then combined together during a meal: a tender green puree made from beet leaves and other herbs, boiled fish and ice chips.

Okroshka	*Okroshka* is another cold soup that is typical in Russian cuisine. It is made with *kvas* as the liquid base, with boiled root vegetables, cucumbers, radishes, herbs and meat added.
Turya	According to the *Explanatory Dictionary of the Living Great Russian Language* by lexicographer Vladimir Dal, *turya* is the simplest of foods. It is composed of pieces of bread soaked in water, *Kvas* (see p. 168) or other liquids, sometimes with addition of other ingredients such as salt and onions. Bread was one of the major staples of the Russian diet and it is likely that *turya* was the major dish of poor households since it was very flexible in terms of necessary ingredients. It is both easy to make and fast to prepare. Despite its popularity in the past, it is now essentially a forgotten dish, as overall consumption of bread has decreased and bread-based dishes have been replaced by other products.

Fresh *Schi*

Schi so svezhei kapustoi

1 lb (500 g) beef (whole brisket is preferred)

10 cups (2.5 L) water

2 cups (500 mL) fresh cabbage, shredded

2 onions, finely chopped

1 potato, diced

1 carrot, diced

1 small turnip, diced

3 black peppercorns

3 bay leaves

2 Tbsp (30 mL) fresh dill, finely chopped

1 cup (250 mL) sour cream

Homemade meat broth is essential for this soup. Both the meat and the broth are used in the preparation. It is important to use fatty pieces of beef to ensure that the broth has a nice flavour and the cooked meat is tender (lean meats can have a rubbery texture). During the long days of Lent in the Russian Orthodox Church calendar, a vegetarian version of *schi* is popular. Mushrooms or fish are used as substitutes for the meat.

Prepare the broth by boiling the entire piece of uncut beef, in water for about an hour. Do not add salt. Skim the foam off the water surface once in a while and discard. After an hour add cabbage, onions, potato, carrot and turnip. Once the soup boils, season with peppercorns and bay leaves and cook on low heat for about 30 minutes until vegetables become tender. Add dill and remove from heat.

Remove peppercorns and bay leaves and serve in soup bowls with a dollop of sour cream.

MAKES 6 SERVINGS

COOKING TIME: 1 HOUR FOR BROTH + 45 MINUTES FOR THE SOUP

Fresh *Schi*, top (p. 84); *Rassolnik*
with Chicken, bottom (p. 91)

Sour S*ʹchi*

Kislie sʹchi

1 lb (500 g) beef (whole brisket is referred)

10 cups (2.5 L) water

1 Tbsp (15 mL) butter

1 onion, finely chopped

1 lb (500 g) Russian Sauerkraut (see p. 77)

2 potatoes, diced

1 carrot, shredded

3–4 dried porcini mushrooms

3 black peppercorns

1 bay leaf

½ cup (125 mL) fresh parsley, chopped

½ cup (125 mL) sour cream

This soup was and still is the most popular soup in Russia. The ingredients are simple and are always available.

Prepare the broth by boiling the entire piece of uncut beef in water. (Do not add salt.) Skim the foam off the water surface once in a while and discard. Drain the broth into a second pot and set the meat aside. Melt butter in a pan and add onion. Drain the sauerkraut and stir fry it with the onion for about 10 to 15 minutes. Set sauerkraut and onion aside. Add the potatoes, carrot and porcini mushrooms to the broth. Add the sauerkraut and onion mixture to the same pot. Once the soup boils, season with peppercorns and bay leaf and cook on low heat for about 45 minutes, until potatoes and carrot are tender. Add parsley and take the pot off the heat. Cut the reserved beef into bite-sized pieces and add to the soup pot. Remove peppercorns and bay leaf and serve in soup bowls with a dollop of sour cream.

MAKES 6 SERVINGS

COOKING TIME: 1 HOUR FOR BROTH PREPARATION + 45 MINUTES FOR THE SOUP

NOTE: To make a vegetarian version of this soup you can omit the meat and use dried mushrooms instead to prepare the base broth. Place about ⅓ cup (80 mL) dry porcini mushrooms in cold water and proceed to add vegetables after the water boils. Do not remove the mushrooms from the soup.

Sorrel *Schi*

Schi s shavlem

———— ❧ ————

1 lb (500 g) beef (whole brisket
   is preferred)

10 cups (2.5 L) water

1 potato, diced

1 carrot, diced

1 onion, finely chopped

1 Tbsp (15 mL) sunflower oil

3 bay leaves

3 black peppercorns

3 cups (750 mL) fresh sorrel,
   finely chopped

2 Tbsp (30 mL) fresh dill,
   finely chopped

1 cup (250 mL) sour cream

This is a typical spring soup. Sorrel was mostly picked in the wild and seldom grown in kitchen gardens.

Prepare the broth by boiling the entire piece of uncut beef in water for about an hour. (Do not add salt.) Skim the foam off the water surface once in a while and discard. Add the potato and carrot to the broth. In a small frying pan, lightly sauté the onion in sunflower oil and then add to the soup. Once the soup boils, season with bay leaves and peppercorns. Cook on a low heat until vegetables are almost tender, about 20 minutes. Add sorrel and fresh dill, cook for an additional 5 to 10 minutes and remove from heat. Remove bay leaves and peppercorns and serve with sour cream.

MAKES 6 SERVINGS

COOKING TIME: 1 HOUR FOR BROTH PREPARATION
+ 45 MINUTES FOR THE SOUP

NOTE: Sorrel is a perennial plant, resembling spinach in appearance with dark green spear-shaped leaves and a distinct sour flavour. It is often used in Eastern European cuisine as an ingredient in soups.

Ukha

———— ❧ ————

1 lb (500 g) zander, dressed (head and tail on)

1 lb (500 g) whitefish, dressed (head and tail on)

10 cups (2.5 L) water, lightly salted

2 potatoes, diced

2 onions, cut in half

1 small carrot, diced

1 parsley root, diced

1 parsnip, diced

1 bay leaf

3 black peppercorns

¼ cup (60 mL) fresh parsley, chopped

¼ cup (60 mL) fresh dill, chopped

salt and pepper to taste

This fish soup is usually made with several types of freshwater fish. Freshness is crucial for the flavour development, so freshly caught fish is preferred whenever possible.

Cut off fish heads and tail and set aside. Remove skin, clean the fish and cut the meat into 1½- to 2-inch (4 to 5 cm) pieces; set aside. Add fish heads and tails to lightly salted boiling water; add potatoes, onions, carrot, parsley root and parsnip. Cook on low heat about for 20 minutes, removing any foam that forms. Add bay leaf and peppercorns and continue cooking for another 5 minutes. Increase heat to medium and add the reserved fish pieces. Cook at a light boil for 15 to 17 minutes. Add parsley and dill. Add salt and pepper to taste. Remove from heat and discard the fish heads and tails and onion pieces. Cover with lid and let the soup stand for about 10 to 15 minutes. Remove bay leaf and peppercorns and discard. Serve hot.

MAKES 6 SERVINGS
PREPARATION TIME: 20 MINUTES
COOKING TIME: 1 HOUR

NOTE: If you cannot find zander you can substitute American walleye or perch.

PARSLEY ROOT

In Russian cuisine, parsley root is often used in cooking. It has a strong parsley flavour and delicate texture and its appearance is similar to that of a parsnip. Sometimes parsley root is dried and added to soups and stews as dry flakes, but when available and in season fresh root is always preferred.

Saltwater *Ukha*

Ukha iz morskoj ribi

1 lb (500 g) cod fillets

1 lb (500 g) sea bass fillets

10 cups (2.5 L) water, lightly salted

3 potatoes, diced

1 small carrot, diced

1 parsley root, diced

1 onion, cut in half

3 bay leaves

5 black peppercorns

1 leek stalk, sliced

1 tsp (5 mL) salt

¼ cup (60 mL) fresh dill, chopped

6 thin slices of lemon

In the past, fish was eaten much more often than meat and salt water fish was not a rarity on the Russian table.

Prepare fish fillets by cutting them into large pieces; about 1½ inches (4 cm) thick and set aside. Bring to a boil 10 cups (2.5 L) lightly salted water. Add potatoes, carrot, parsley root and onion and cook for 15 minutes on medium heat. Add bay leaves, peppercorns, leek and salt and cook for an additional 3 minutes. Add fish fillet pieces and continue cooking for 10 to 15 minutes. Add dill. Remove pot from heat, and discard onion pieces. Cover with lid and let the soup stand for 10 minutes. Remove bay leaves and peppercorns and discard. To serve, ladle *ukha* into soup bowls and garnish with lemon slices. Serve hot.

MAKES 6 SERVINGS

PREPARATION TIME: 20 MINUTES

COOKING TIME: 1 HOUR

MY MOTHER'S MEMOIR: *Cod Fishing*

Once I was invited to go fishing for cod in the White Sea. It was a very important event that required ample preparations the day before—we had to find a boat and prepare all the fishing equipment. At dawn we set out into the open sea on a tiny boat with some oars and fishing rods at the bottom of the boat. We were almost at the fishing spot when we noticed that we forgot the bait. It was useless to head back to the shore as we would miss the time when fish was ready to bite. We were sad and disappointed but then one of the oarsmen asked if anyone had a piece of red fabric we could try tying to the hook. Luckily we found a piece of red fabric in one of our pockets and tied a little piece of it to the hook. What a surprise it was when a huge cod immediately pulled the hook with the red piece tied to it right under our boat! We caught quite a bit of cod with this method until we ran out of fabric. Then someone suggested that maybe we should just throw the bare hook one last time before heading back home. To our great surprise the biggest cod we'd seen so far was eager to swallow the shiny object.

Only later on the shore, when we were all enjoying our dinner of cod ukha, did we discover that it was all a trick. All novice fishers were taken to that fishing spot not knowing that cod are attracted by such odd things as red pieces of fabric or shiny metal hooks. Nevertheless the soup turned out great and its lovely aroma was unforgettable.

Rassolnik with Chicken

Rassolnik s kuricei

½ whole chicken, about 2 lb (½ kg)

10 cups (2.5 L) water

1 large carrot, diced

1 medium potato, diced

1 parsley root, diced

3 Tbsp (15 mL) rice

1 medium onion, finely chopped

1 leek stalk, sliced

3 black peppercorns

2 bay leaves

4 dill pickles (in salt brine only, no vinegar), finely chopped

2 Tbsp (30 mL) fresh dill, finely chopped

⅓ bunch fresh parsley, finely chopped

1 Tbsp (15 mL) thyme (fresh or dry)

2 garlic cloves, crushed

3 Tbsp (45 mL) butter

1 tsp (5 mL) salt

6 Tbsp (90 mL) sour cream

Although soups based on salt brine from pickled vegetables (mostly cabbage and cucumber) were known in Russia as early as 15th century, *rassolnik* was developed relatively late, in the middle of the 19th century. *Rassolnik* has a distinctive sour-salty taste and always contains cucumbers pickled in brine (never in vinegar). *Rassolnik* often contains potatoes and rice—relatively new foods for traditional Russian cuisine. Grains for the *rassolnik* are coordinated with the type of meat used for the broth base: if kidneys and beef are used, then barley is added; if chicken or turkey is used, then rice is added. For Lent versions of *rassolnik* where a vegetarian broth is used, rice or buckwheat is added. *Rassolnik* is usually served with sour cream.

Clean and cut the chicken, leaving skin on and bones in, and place it in a large pot filled with 10 cups (2.5L) of water. Bring to a boil, and cook on medium heat for about an hour, removing any foam that accumulates on top. Add carrot, potato, parsley root and rice. Cook until rice is al dente, removing the foam from time to time. Add onion, leek, peppercorns and bay leaves, and continue cooking until rice is soft. Add pickles, dill, parsley and thyme; cook for another 3 to 5 minutes. Remove the pot from heat and stir in the crushed garlic, butter and salt. Remove peppercorns and bay leaves and serve in soup bowls with a dollop of sour cream.

MAKES 6 SERVINGS

PREPARATION TIME: 20 MINUTES

COOKING TIME: 1 HOUR FOR BROTH + 45 MINUTES FOR THE SOUP

NOTE: To prepare the vegetarian version of the *rassolnik* follow the same procedure as in the *Rassolnik* with Chicken but omit the chicken and use a larger potato, 3 dill pickles, ¼ bunch of parsley and reduce cooking time to 30 minutes—just until the potato and buckwheat (or rice) become soft.

Solyanka with Mushrooms

Solyanka s gribami

8 dried boletus or porcini
  mushrooms

10 cups (2.5 L) water

1 carrot, julienned

1 parsley root, julienned

1 small celery root, julienned

2 Tbsp (30 mL) butter

2 cups (500 mL) finely chopped
  fresh cabbage

1½ cups (375 mL) sauerkraut,
  drained (see p. 77)

2 tomatoes, chopped

2 onions, chopped

½ cup (125 mL) smoked sausage,
  diced (optional)

¼ cup (60 mL) mortadella sausage,
  diced (optional)

¼ cup (60 mL) ham, diced
  (optional)

10 black olives

juice of ½ lemon

6 Tbsp (90 mL) sour cream

¼ cup (60 mL) fresh dill, chopped

Solyanka belongs to a special soup category, where the liquid (broth) and the solids (vegetables and meat) are cooked separately and assembled at the last moment, just before serving. The name "*solyanka*" comes from the word *sol*, meaning salt, the main ingredient in the dish that comes from the salt-brined vegetables (cabbage, cucumbers or mushrooms). There are three types of this salty-sour soup: meat, fish and mushroom based. *Solyanka* usually has less liquid than other Russian soups, giving it a rich stew-like consistency.

In a large pot, boil the dried mushrooms in water. With a slotted spoon, remove the mushrooms when they become soft after about 20 minutes, chop them finely and return them to the broth. Add julienned carrot, parsley and celery root and cook for about 20 minutes. In a deep frying pan, melt butter and sauté fresh cabbage, sauerkraut, tomatoes and onions until tender. Add the sautéed mixture to the pot; if using, add smoked sausage, mortadella sausage and ham with the broth and julienned vegetables. Keep the pot on low heat for another 10 minutes. Remove from heat, add olives and lemon juice. Serve in bowls with a dollop of sour cream and some dill.

MAKES 6 SERVINGS
PREPARATION TIME: 30 MINUTES
COOKING TIME: 1 HOUR

NOTE: For a vegetarian version of this dish omit the sausage and ham and include 10 additional olives.

Mushroom *Pokhlebka*

Gribnaya pokhlebka

10 cups (2.5 L) water

⅓ cup (80 mL) dried porcini
 mushrooms

¼ cup (60 mL) pearl barley

2 medium potatoes, diced

3 Tbsp (45 mL) sunflower oil

1 medium onion, diced

1 carrot, shredded

1 tsp (5 mL) sugar

¼ tsp (1 mL) black pepper

½ tsp (2 mL) salt

1 Tbsp (15 mL) fresh dill, chopped

1 Tbsp (15 mL) fresh parsley,
 chopped

Pokhlebka is a rich and hearty soup that is perfect for cold autumn and winter days. Dry mushrooms give this soup a wonderful rich colour and aroma.

In slightly salted water bring mushrooms to a boil, add barley, diced potatoes and lower heat to medium-low. In a separate frying pan, heat the oil and add the onion, carrot and sugar. Sauté until the onions are lightly browned. Add the carrot and onion mixture to the pot, along with the black pepper and salt. Continue cooking until barley is tender. Add dill and parsley and remove from heat. Serve with a dollop of sour cream on each soup bowl.

MAKES 6 SERVINGS
PREPARATION TIME: 20 MINUTES
COOKING TIME: 40 MINUTES

Mushroom Noodle Soup

Sup s lapshei i gribami

NOODLES

1 egg

1¼ cups (310 mL) all-purpose flour, divided

3–4 Tbsp (45–60 mL) water

¼ tsp (1 mL) salt

BROTH

6 dried porcini mushrooms

10 cups (2.5 L) water

1 medium carrot, diced

1 onion, diced

4 black peppercorns

3 bay leaves

1 tsp (5 mL) salt

¼ cup (60 mL) fresh dill, chopped

2 garlic cloves, minced

Noodle soup was most likely introduced to the European part of Russia by the Tatars. The characteristic trait of this soup is long noodles made from basic dough, cooked in different broths.

NOODLES

In a large bowl, combine egg, 1 cup (250 mL) flour, water and salt and stir well until a firm dough is formed. Cover the dough with a clean tea towel and let it rest for about 10 minutes. Dust a large, clean work surface with the remaining flour and roll out the dough into a very thin sheet, no more than ⅛ inch (3 mm). With a very sharp knife, cut the dough into long thin strips about ⅛ inch (3 mm) wide. Scatter the dough strips on a clean tea towel and let them dry slightly while the broth is cooking.

BROTH

Place the mushrooms in a large saucepan with cold water and bring it to a boil. Add the carrot and onion. Once the mushrooms soften (about 20 minutes), add the noodles to the boiling broth. Add peppercorns and bay leaves and cook until noodles are tender. Add salt, dill and garlic and remove from heat. Remove peppercorns and bay leaves and discard.

MAKES 6 SERVINGS

PREPARATION TIME: 30 MINUTES

COOKING TIME: 30 MINUTES

Botvinia

Botvinia is a very old Russian cold soup recipe made here with sorrel and salmon. It is perfect for hot summer days and is served in three parts, on three separate plates: the soup, the fish and the ice. Horseradish is a typical condiment and is also served separately. This dish requires the use of two spoons and a fork.

2 cups (500 mL) peeled, diced (bite-size) cucumber

4 cups (1 L) in total of fresh sorrel, beet greens, young nettle (optional) and spinach

two 1 lb (500 g) salmon fillets, bones removed, skin on

¼ cup (60 mL) parsley

4 cups (1 L) *Kvas* (see p. 168)

⅓ cup (80 mL) each: fresh dill, tarragon and parsley

2 cups (500 mL) ice chips, divided

1 tsp (5 mL) sugar

2 tsp (10 mL) salt

¼ cup (60 mL) horseradish, grated

Place the cucumber in a bowl and refrigerate. Clean the sorrel, beet greens, young nettle and spinach, and blanch in a large pot of boiling, salted water, for 2 to 3 minutes. Drain and purée in a blender or food processor, or chop very finely and set aside. In a saucepan, boil the salmon in salted water (enough water to cover the fish) until fully cooked through (about 20 minutes); drain and chill for about an hour until the fish is completely cold and place on a serving plate. Garnish with parsley. In a separate deep soup plate combine herb puree with cucumber and *kvas*, garnish with finely chopped dill, tarragon, parsley and several ice chips. Season with sugar and salt to taste.

Serve with salmon and horseradish on the side and a bowl of ice chips. The proper way of eating the *botvinia* is to keep adding the ice chips into the herb soup while eating it with salmon in order to keep it as cold as possible.

MAKES 4 SERVINGS
PREPARATION TIME: 20 MINUTES
COOKING TIME: 30 MINUTES + 1 HOUR FOR FISH TO CHILL

Okroshka

———— ❧ ————

3 potatoes, whole

3 eggs, hard-boiled, finely chopped

1 small bunch radishes, thinly sliced

4 fresh cucumbers, thinly sliced

½ bunch green onions, finely
   chopped

½ bunch fresh dill, finely chopped

8 cups (2 L) *Kvas* (see p. 168)

1 tsp (5 mL) salt

1 tsp (5 mL) black pepper

3 Tbsp (45 mL) sour cream

Okroshka is a cold, light soup, perfect for hot summer days and made from *kvas*, vegetables and eggs. Its simple ingredients made it a favourite in both the 19th century and in the Soviet period.

Boil the potatoes until tender, let them cool and remove the skins. Finely dice the potatoes and place them into a deep serving pot or bowl (soup tureen will work well). Add eggs, radishes, cucumbers, green onions and dill. Add *kvas* to the pot, season with salt and pepper and mix well. Chill in refrigerator for at least 1 hour. To serve, ladle the chilled *okroshka* into soup plates and add a dollop of sour cream to each plate.

MAKES 4 SERVINGS

PREPARATION TIME: 20 MINUTES

COOKING TIME: 1 HOUR TO CHILL

NOTE: To prepare this dish in advance, refrigerate all the ingredients until needed and add *kvas* right before serving. Salt causes the *kvas* to fizz, so some foaming is normal

NOTE: In order to get the most enjoyment out of this dish it is important not only to select the right ingredients but also the time and place for eating. *Okroshka* tastes best when it is eaten on a hot summer day, in open air (on the deck in your yard or on a picnic in the park) under a shady tree.

Main Meals

RADITIONAL RUSSIAN MEALS can be roughly divided into three categories: meat-based dishes, fish-based dishes and plant-based dishes. The choice of a main course dish was usually heavily influenced by seasonality of the products used in preparation of this dish, as well as the church calendar that indicated which days one can eat meat, fish or vegetables. Kashas and savoury *pirogi*, such as *Kurnik* (see p. 143) or *koulebyaka* (see p. 140), were also often served as a main course dish.

Russian main meals are usually served after the soup. Soup was regarded as the main component of the whole meal and all other dishes such as appetizers, main courses and desserts were usually selected to accompany a particular soup and not the other way around. For special occasions, more than one main dish would be served.

Boiled Beef with Horseradish

Otvarnaya govyadina s hrenom

1 lb (500 g) beef, in one piece
  (brisket or shoulder)
½ Tbsp (7 mL) salt
1 large carrot, diced
1 small onion, cut into thick wedges
2 bay leaves
1 tsp (5 mL) black peppercorns
2 lb (1 kg) potatoes, whole, peeled

SAUCE

4 Tbsp (60 mL) butter, divided
1 Tbsp (15 mL) all-purpose flour
½ cup (125 mL) beef or vegetable
  broth (reserved)
½ cup (125 mL) sour cream
2 Tbsp (30 mL) fresh horseradish,
  grated
1 Tbsp (15 mL) vinegar
¼ tsp (1 mL) salt

This hearty dish is perfect for a winter dinner.

Clean the meat and place it in a large stockpot filled with enough cold water to cover the entire piece—about 8 cups (2 L). Cover the pot with a lid and bring to a boil. Remove any foam that forms on the surface. Add salt, and continue cooking on a low heat for 1½ hours. Add carrot, onion, bay leaves and peppercorns and continue to cook for another 30 minutes, or until vegetables are tender. Remove from heat and discard bay leaves and peppercorns; reserve ½ cup (125 mL) broth for the sauce preparation.

In a separate pot, boil the potatoes in lightly salted water until tender (about 20 to 30 minutes).

While the potatoes are cooking, make the sauce. In a small saucepan, melt 2 Tbsp (30 mL) butter and then add the flour, whisking the mixture until the flour becomes lightly browned. Add the ½ cup (125 mL) reserved broth, continue whisking and gradually add the sour cream. Continue heating for another 10 to 15 minutes. In a separate saucepan, melt the remaining butter, add horseradish and vinegar, and heat for 3 to 5 minutes. Add the horseradish mix and salt to the sauce and bring mixture to a boiling point before removing from heat. Set aside; warm up when ready to serve.

To serve, thinly slice the meat and arrange on a serving platter together with cooked vegetables from the broth and the boiled potatoes. Pour the horseradish sauce over the serving platter or serve separately.

MAKES 6 SERVINGS
PREPARATION TIME: 30 MINUTES
COOKING TIME: 2½ HOURS

NOTE: This cooking method is also used to prepare *solonina* (meat preserved in salt). In the past, before refrigeration, meat was often heavily salted to keep it fresh for long periods of time. Before cooking, the meat had to be presoaked in fresh water for several hours in order to remove excess salt.

Pelmeni

DOUGH

5 cups (1.25 L) all-purpose flour

1 tsp (5 mL) salt

1 egg

1 cup (250 mL) water

FILLING

½ lb (250 g) ground beef

½ lb (250 g) ground pork

1 large cooking onion, finely minced

½ tsp (2 mL) sugar

1 tsp (5 mL) salt

1 tsp (5 mL) black pepper

1 cup (250 mL) butter, melted

NOTE: Like blini, *pelmeni* are usually served in large quantities and require special condiments. In addition to melted butter, sour cream, light vinegar and freshly ground black pepper are the usual accompaniments.

Although these meat dumplings are readily available in commercially made frozen packages, people still prefer the homemade version. Making *pelmeni* is quite time consuming, so it is often a family affair, with several members of the household involved in the preparation. This beloved Russian dish was also very popular during the Soviet period.

On a clean flat surface, mound the flour and make a well in the middle. Add salt, egg and water to the well and gradually stir in the flour to make a firm dough. Knead well for about 5 minutes, and then let rest under a clean tea towel for about 20 minutes.

In the meantime, make the filling by combining the ground beef and pork in a bowl with the minced onion, sugar, salt and pepper. Mix well.

After the dough has rested, divide it into 2 equal parts and form into rounds. On a well-floured surface roll out each piece into ¹⁄₁₆ inch (1.5 mm) thin sheets. Using a small round cookie cutter or a round cup make dough rounds for the *pelmeni*. Place about 1 tsp (5 mL) filling in the middle of each dough round, fold in half and pinch the edges tightly, giving *pelmeni* a half-moon shape. Then, pinch the corners together to make the final ring shape. If the edges do not stick well, brush with a little bit of water to make the dough sticky. Place the finished *pelmeni* on a cutting board dusted with flour and continue until all dough is used up. At this point, *pelmeni* may be cooked right away or placed in the freezer for future use.

To cook, bring a large stockpot full of salted water to a rolling boil (3 Tbsp [45 mL]) salt is needed for every litre of water). Cook *pelmeni* in small batches for about 5 to 7 minutes on medium heat. Remove them from the water with a slotted spoon and place in a serving bowl. Drizzle with melted butter and serve hot.

MAKES 10 SERVINGS

PREPARATION TIME: 1 HOUR

COOKING TIME: 20 MINUTES

Pork and Chicken in Aspic

Studen

— ❦ —

1 pork foot or hock

one 4.4 lb (2 kg) soup chicken, whole

1 large onion, whole and peeled

2 large carrots, 1 whole and 1 decoratively sliced (see p. 103)

10 black peppercorns

2 bay leaves

salt to taste

1 Tbsp (15 mL) strong mustard

1 Tbsp (15 mL) strong horseradish

3 sprigs of fresh parsley

3 sprigs of fresh dill

This ancient dish is still frequently made for special occasions. In our family, it is served with mustard and horseradish dressings on the side. It is very important to use an old chicken (soup chicken) in this recipe.

Clean the pork foot thoroughly. Pour cold water into a large stockpot (8 cups [2 L] of water for every 2 lb [1 kg] of meat). Add the pork and the chicken to the pot, along with the whole onion, whole carrot and peppercorns. Slow cook on a low heat for about 4 hours. One hour before the end of cooking, remove the carrot and onion. Add the decoratively sliced carrot, bay leaves and salt. When the meat comes off the bones easily, remove pork and chicken from the broth.

Detach the meat from both the chicken and the pork, cut it up in small pieces, and reserve. Strain the broth and reserve the sliced carrots.

In a deep dish, place the carrot slices on the bottom, add a layer of meat and pour in all the broth. Let the dish set overnight in the refrigerator.

Studen is typically served cold, in slices, with a strong mustard and horseradish, and garnished with fresh parsley and dill.

MAKES 8 SERVINGS

PREPARATION TIME: 20 MINUTES

COOKING TIME: 4 HOURS + OVERNIGHT TO SET

ASPIC

Aspic is a traditional Russian dish where vegetables and meat are set in gelatin made from a strong meat broth. Typically pork, beef or chicken are used to make aspic. Old chicken is a better source of gelatin than a young one and that is why, for this recipe, it is best to use an older chicken (also known as soup chicken). When cooled down the strong broth jellifies and becomes solid and transparent, so it can be sliced. Aspic is a very attractive dish and is often served for special occasions.

Sturgeon in Aspic

Zalivnaya osertrina

⸺◦◦⋆◦◦⸺

one 4.4 lb (2 kg) sturgeon, dressed,
   head and tail on
2 cups (500 mL) clear fish stock
   (approx.), divided
1 medium onion, cut into wedges
1 medium carrot, decoratively sliced
1 parsley root, decoratively sliced
4 whole black peppercorns
1 tsp (5 mL) salt
1 large bay leaf
½ lemon, thinly sliced
2 hard-boiled eggs, sliced
¼ cup (60 mL) olives

Fish cooked in the shape of a ring is an ancient method of preparation. Wood carvings depicting ring-shaped fish motifs can be found on old Russian kitchen items such as cutting boards, looms and gingerbread press boards.

Clean and rinse the sturgeon. Bend the fish into a circle shape, so that the head touches the tail, and place on the bottom of a deep, heatproof dish. Completely cover the sturgeon with fish stock. Add the onion, carrot and parsley root. Season with peppercorns, salt and bay leaf. Cook on a stovetop on low heat for about 40 minutes with liquid gently simmering, until fish cooks through; the flesh should be uniformly opaque in colour with no translucency and should flake easily.

Once the fish is ready, carefully place it on a serving dish, keeping the ring shape. Glaze with remaining stock right away (it will turn gelatinous once it has completely cooled down), and decorate with slices of lemon, eggs, olives and root vegetables from the broth. Refrigerate for at least an hour to let the stock set completely.

MAKES 8 SERVINGS
PREPARATION TIME: 20 MINUTES
COOKING TIME: 40 MINUTES + 1 HOUR TO SET

DECORATIVE VEGETABLE CUTTING

A great way to give a personal touch to your dish is through cutting the ingredients in a visually appealing shape. Carrots for example can be sliced on an angle producing oval thin slices, or cut into flower shapes by carving 4 to 5 lengthwise dents along the carrot and then slicing it as usual. Nicely-cut vegetables that are used for garnish in main meals can make the dish more attractive, so use your imagination and experiment with different ways of cutting your vegetables.

Pozharsky Cutlets

Pozharskie kotleti

4 chicken breasts, skinless

3 Tbsp (45 mL) unsalted butter, softened

2 slices French white bread, crust removed

1 tsp (5 mL) salt

1 tsp (5 mL) black pepper

½ cup (125 mL) cream (18%)

1 egg, lightly beaten

1 cup (250 mL) bread crumbs (approx.)

The addition of breadcrumbs and cream make these Pozharsky cutlets very moist and tender.

Grind the chicken breasts in a meat grinder or food processor and transfer into a large mixing bowl. Add softened butter, bread, salt and pepper and enough cream to make a soft mass. Mix all ingredients thoroughly and let the mixture rest for 15 to 20 minutes.

Pinch off a small amount of the mixture, about the size of a plum, and shape it into an oblong cutlet, about ¼ inch (6 mm) thick. Repeat the process with the rest of the mixture and make sure the cutlets are more or less same size and thickness. Coat with lightly beaten egg and bread crumbs, and pan fry in butter for about 10 minutes on both sides until golden brown and thoroughly cooked. Serve the cutlets hot with a light salad or boiled seasonal vegetables.

MAKES 4 SERVINGS
PREPARATION TIME: 20 MINUTES
COOKING TIME: 30 MINUTES

MY MOTHER'S MEMOIR: *Goose with Apples*

My mother [author's grandmother] would often buy a whole goose with the feathers on. She plucked the feathers and used them to stuff pillows and rendered goose fat to be used in baking and cooking. Goose heart, liver and neck and the tips of wings were used to prepare rassolnik *(see* *p. 91**). It was delicious! The rest of the goose was well stuffed with buckwheat kasha, sewn up and slowly roasted, filling the entire house with wonderful aromas.*

Roasted Goose with Apples and Buckwheat Stuffing

Gus zapechennij s yablokami i grechnevoy kashei

6 large apples, divided

2 cups (500 mL) cooked buckwheat

2 tsp (10 mL) salt

1 medium goose (about 7 lb [3.2 kg])

2½ cups (625 mL) chicken or
   vegetable broth

¼ cup (60 mL) sugar

This festive dish can be also made with rice or wheat berries instead of buckwheat.

Core one apple and slice into bite-sized pieces; do not peel. Mix the apple slices with buckwheat and salt and set aside. Preheat the oven to 400°F (200°C). Clean the goose and carefully stuff it with buckwheat and apple mixture. Sew or tie up the opening and place the goose in a deep baking tray. Rub the goose with cold water to prevent the skin from burning and place the tray into the preheated oven. Once the skin browns a bit and most of the fat melts, remove from the oven, drain the fat from the tray and set the fat aside. Add the broth to the bottom of the tray and return to the oven. Reduce the heat to 350°F (175°C) and continue cooking for about 2 to 2 ½ hours (depending on the size of the goose). Don't forget to frequently baste the goose with the liquid from the bottom of the tray.

Keeping the skins on, core and slice the remaining apples. Arrange them carefully in an ovenproof saucepan or ceramic dish, dust with sugar, drizzle with a bit of the reserved goose fat and bake until tender (about 5 to 10 minutes).

Once the goose is completely cooked, remove it from the oven, place on a large serving dish and arrange the baked apples around it. Pour some of the juice from the tray over the apples and goose, and serve the rest separately as a sauce. Serve immediately, while the goose is still very hot.

MAKES 6 SERVINGS

PREPARATION TIME: 40 MINUTES

COOKING TIME: 3 HOURS

Steamed Sterlet with Bouquet Garni

Parovaya sterlyad

one 5 lb (2.2 kg) medium sterlet,
   dressed, head and tail on
1½ cups (375 mL) white wine
2 cup (500 mL) fish broth
1 parsley root, julienned
1 parsnip, julienned
1 bouquet garni (dried or fresh)
   (see p. 107)
4 sprigs of fresh parsley
5 thin slices of lemon

Sterlet is a separate species of sturgeon, native to Russia. In the past this fish was available in large quantities and was widely used in Russian traditional cuisine.

Sterlet is not native to North America, but can be found at some specialty stores. If you are unable to find it you may substitute with a similar sized sturgeon.

This dish goes well with steamed asparagus or a light salad.

Bend the sterlet into a ring shape and attach the head to the tail with thread. Place on a wire mesh inside a large stockpot. Add wine, broth, parsley root, parsnip and garni, and steam under closed lid, on medium heat, until fish cooks through (about 30 minutes). When done, carefully remove the skin and transfer the fish to a serving plate, keeping the ring shape. Garnish with parsley and lemon slices.

The broth can be used to prepare a sauce to accompany the fish (see below), and the root vegetables can be served on the side.

MAKES 6 SERVINGS
PREPARATION TIME: 20 MINUTES
COOKING TIME: 30 MINUTES

Sauce for Steamed Sterlet

Sous k parovoi sterlyadi

1 shallot, finely diced
6 Tbsp (90 mL) white wine (or
   3 Tbsp [45 mL] white wine +
   3 Tbsp [45 mL] sterlet broth)
1 Tbsp (15 mL) sour cream
½ cup (125 mL) + 2 Tbsp (30 mL)
   butter
½ tsp (2 mL) salt
½ tsp (2 mL) black pepper

In a small saucepan combine diced shallot with white wine and broth (if using) and heat gently until liquid starts to bubble at the edges. Reduce heat to low and whisk in sour cream. While whisking slowly add butter to get a smooth even texture. Season with salt and pepper and keep the sauce warm until serving.

MAKES 1 CUP
PREPARATION TIME: 15 MINUTES

Steamed Trout with Butter Sauce

Parovaja porcionnaja forel s maslyanim sousom

one 1 lb (500 g) rainbow trout,
dressed, head and tail removed,
skin on
1 bouquet garni
1½ cups (375 mL) white wine
2 cups (500 mL) fish stock

SAUCE

½ cup (125 ml) butter + 2 Tbsp
(30 mL) softened butter, divided
2 Tbsp (30 mL) flour
2½ cups (625 mL) cooking liquid
(reserved)
2 egg yolks
1 Tbsp (15 mL) lemon juice
Pinch of cayenne powder (optional)
2 Tbsp (30 mL) fresh dill, finely
chopped

Try this recipe for a light dinner on a warm summer weekend.

Cut the trout into portion-sized pieces and place on a wire mesh inside a large stockpot. Add bouquet garni, white wine and fish stock, cover with lid, and cook on medium heat until fish cooks through (about 30 minutes). Once done, reserve about 2½ cups (625 mL) cooking liquid for the sauce. Place the fish pieces on serving plates.

To prepare the sauce, melt ½ cup (125 mL) butter in a small saucepan. Gradually add the flour, whisking constantly. Continue whisking, add the reserved cooking liquid and simmer on low heat until sauce thickens. In a small bowl, mix together egg yolks, 2 Tbsp (30 mL) softened butter, lemon juice and cayenne pepper, and add to the saucepan. Continue cooking for a few more minutes, stirring frequently, until sauce thickens a bit more. Add finely chopped dill and remove from heat and serve in a sauceboat or pour directly over fish before serving.

MAKES 4 SERVINGS
PREPARATION TIME: 15 MINUTES
COOKING TIME: 40 MINUTES

BOUQUET GARNI

Bouquet garni is a bundle of dried aromatic herbs that is added to the broth to give it extra flavour. Typically these herbs are bound with a string or placed into a small cheesecloth bag, so they can be removed after cooking. A traditional bouquet garni contains bay leaves, thyme and rosemary. For fish it could also contain cilantro, basil, fennel and parsley. You can make your own combination by tying together some dried herbs with a twine or placing them into a cheesecloth bundle, or you can buy already prepared bouquet garni in the store.

Trout and Potato Pots

Forel v gorshochkah

two ½ lb (250 g) rainbow trout
  fillets, skin removed
2 potatoes, peeled and diced
1 small carrot, diced
1 medium onion, sliced into rings
4 whole black peppercorns
4 bay leafs
1 tsp (5 mL) salt
¾ cup (185 mL) water
¼ cup (60 mL) fresh parsley,
  chopped
¼ cup (60 mL) fresh dill, chopped

This dish is cooked and served in individual portion-sized ceramic pots (*gorshochki*) with lids, and makes a wonderful main course on a cold day.

Preheat oven to 350°F (175°C).

Cut the trout into bite-sized pieces and place 3 to 4 pieces in each of the four ceramic pots. Divide the diced potatoes, carrot and sliced onion among the pots. Add a peppercorn and bay leaf to each pot, and sprinkle with salt. Pour about 3 Tbsp (45 mL) water into each pot. Cover pots with lids, place on a baking sheet and put in preheated oven for 30 to 40 minutes, until fish cooks through and vegetables are tender. If you do not have lids, cover the top of the pot with aluminum foil to prevent top layer from drying out.

Remove the pots from the oven, clean sides (some broth may have spilled during cooking), sprinkle each pot with parsley and dill and serve immediately.

MAKES 4 SERVINGS
PREPARATION TIME: 25 MINUTES
COOKING TIME: 40 MINUTES

GORSHOCHKI

Gorschochki are a typical type of cooking pot that were used to cook foods in the Russian oven. They were made out of clay or metal and had a particular shape with a narrow bottom and a wider top. They came in a variety of sizes, from large enough to cook a full family meal to smaller individual sized pots. While the bigger ones are no longer used (as Russian ovens are no longer the rulers of the kitchens), the individual portion-sized small gorshochki survived and are now used to bake small portions of food, or used to serve the food piping hot right out of the oven.

Beet and Sour Cream Pots

Svekla v smetane v gorshochkah

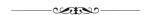

3 large beets, skin on
½ cup (125 mL) sour cream (30%)
1 tsp (5 mL) salt

Traditionally this dish is cooked and served in *gorshochki* (see p. 108). It is a typical dish of the town of Suzdal. Suzdal is located in the Golden Ring area—a chain of beautiful small and ancient towns surrounding Moscow.

Place beets in a deep saucepan, cover with cold water and cook until they are easily pierced with a knife, about 40 to 50 minutes. Once cooked, drain the water, let cool just enough to handle contents, peel the beets and shred them using a large cheese grater or a food processor.

Preheat oven to 350°F (175°C). Place the beets into four portion-sized ceramic pots, filling them about two-thirds full. To each pot, add equal amounts of sour cream and salt, and mix well. Cover the pots with lids and place in preheated oven for 30 to 40 minutes. Remove from oven and serve immediately.

MAKES 4 SERVINGS
PREPARATION TIME: 1 HOUR
COOKING TIME: 40 MINUTES

Baked Eggs

Drochena

4 eggs
1 tsp (5 mL) flour
3 Tbsp (45 mL) butter, divided
½ cup (125 mL) milk, lukewarm

Drochena was traditionally eaten with rye bread.

Preheat oven to 400°F (200°C).

In a mixing bowl, combine eggs with flour. Add 1 Tbsp (15 mL) melted butter and blend well. Gradually, while whisking, add lukewarm milk. Pour the mixture into a well-greased cast iron pan or ovenproof dish and bake for about 15 to 20 minutes. Remove from oven, melt the remaining 2 Tbsp (30 mL) butter and drizzle on top of the eggs. Serve immediately.

MAKES 4 SERVINGS
PREPARATION TIME: 10 MINUTES
COOKING TIME: 20 MINUTES

Turnips Stuffed with Cream of Wheat

Repa farshirovannaja mannoi kashei

4 turnips, peeled
⅓ cup (80 mL) Cream of Wheat,
    cooked in milk
4 tsp (20 mL) fresh parsley, minced
½ cup (125 mL) grated cheese,
    such as mozzarella
¼ cup (60 mL) melted butter

This dish can be served by itself as a main course or as a side to meat or fish.

In a saucepan, cover the turnips with water and boil until tender, about 15 minutes. Drain, and let cool.

Preheat oven to 400°F (200°C).

Once turnips are cooled, cut off the top third of each. With a teaspoon, carefully remove most of the inner flesh, leaving a hollow. Using a food processor or a blender, puree the turnip flesh and mix with Cream of Wheat and parsley. Fill the turnips with this mixture and arrange in an ovenproof ceramic dish. Sprinkle the turnips with grated cheese and drizzle with melted butter. Place turnips in the oven and bake until cheese melts and turns golden, about 30 minutes.

Serve hot as a main dish or as a side.

MAKES 4 SERVINGS
PREPARATION TIME: 20 MINUTES
COOKING TIME: 15 MINUTES

NOTE: You can also stuff turnips with ground pork or beef instead of the Cream of Wheat and cook them in the same manner.

Turnips with Green Peas

Repa s zelenim goroshkom

4 turnips, peeled and cut into
½-inch (1 cm) rounds

5 Tbsp (75 mL) butter, melted,
divided

¼ cup (60 mL) chicken broth,
strongly flavoured

1 cup (250 mL) green peas, shelled

1 small garlic clove, chopped

¼ cup (60 mL) whipping cream
(35%)

½ tsp (2 mL) salt

This recipe was first described in detail for home cooking purposes by Pelageya Alexandrova-Ignatieva, author of the first major cooking manual for domestic use. The recipe survived with no changes until well into the 1960s and was reprinted in Soviet era cook books.

Place turnip rounds into a saucepan, cover with water, and boil until they can be pierced easily with a knife, but are still firm, about 5 minutes. Drain, and let cool.

Preheat oven to 400°F (200°C).

With a teaspoon, scrape some of the flesh from the middle of each round, leaving a little dimple. Arrange turnip rounds in a shallow ovenproof ceramic or glass dish. Drizzle with ¼ cup (60 mL) melted butter and the chicken broth, and bake in oven until tender, about 10 minutes.

Meanwhile, in a saucepan, cook the green peas in lightly salted water until tender. Drain and transfer to a frying pan, adding the garlic and remaining 1 Tbsp (15 mL) melted butter. Fry until garlic becomes aromatic. Remove from heat and stir in the whipping cream.

Spoon the pea mixture into the dimple of each turnip round and serve hot.

MAKES 6 SERVINGS
PREPARATION TIME: 15 MINUTES
COOKING TIME: 30 MINUTES

Kasha

RADITIONAL, OLD COOKED GRAIN OR KASHA recipes were complex and required many ingredients, particularly whole grains. Typically, kashas were prepared overnight, letting the grains and other ingredients slowly steam and bake in cast iron or clay pots inside a traditional Russian oven. With the move from the Russian oven to stovetop preparation, starting in the late 19th century, many ingredients were omitted and recipes were significantly simplified to suit modern needs. The recipes in this chapter are the traditional forms, though they are still enjoyed today.

Wild Mushroom and Roasted Buckwheat Kasha

Grechnevaya kasha s gribami

1 cup (250 mL) buckwheat

2 cups (500 mL) water

¼ cup (60 mL) butter

1 small onion, diced

1 cup (250 mL) wild mushrooms, chopped

½ tsp (2 mL) salt

½ tsp (2 mL) black pepper

Typically wild mushrooms that are picked in the forest are used for this recipe. In winter dried mushrooms could be used. You can use oyster mushrooms or chanterelles in this recipe if you do not have access to wild mushrooms.

Place buckwheat in a dry frying pan and roast on high heat, stirring constantly until kernels start to pop, about 5 minutes. Immediately remove from heat, transfer the buckwheat to a saucepan, add water and simmer on low heat until all liquid is absorbed and kernels are tender, about 15 to 20 minutes.

Meanwhile, in a separate frying pan, melt the butter and sauté the onion and mushrooms until onion is golden. Season with salt and pepper. Transfer the onion and mushroom mix to the buckwheat, mix well and serve hot.

MAKES 4 SERVINGS
PREPARATION TIME: 10 MINUTES
COOKING TIME: 30 MINUTES

Millet Kasha

Pshennaya kasha

———— ❦ ————

1 cup (250 mL) millet
2½ cups (625 mL) water
⅓ tsp (2 mL) salt
3 Tbsp (45 mL) butter

This is one of the staple dishes of Russian cuisine. Millet can be found in any Russian kitchen pantry.

In a fine sieve, rinse millet under cold running water until water runs clear. Place millet in a saucepan with water and cook on low heat until all liquid is absorbed and millet grains are tender, about 20 minutes. When ready, remove from heat, add salt and butter, and mix well. Serve hot.

MAKES 4 SERVINGS
PREPARATION TIME: 10 MINUTES
COOKING TIME: 20 MINUTES

MY MOTHER'S MEMOIR: *Borscht and Millet Kasha*

My mother [author's grandmother] prepared a wide variety of borscht soups: with white beans, with chicken, with beef, with pork fat, with sunflower oil, with haluski (thick soft noodles) or our favorite—with millet kasha.

Year after year, the appearance and the flavour of these soups remained constant, and even if she could not find the exact ingredients she made corrections to make sure that borscht with a particular filling still tasted the way it always did.

Borscht with kasha is very filling and satisfying. Usually my mother would cook it in the summer in her kitchen. When she made vegetarian borscht with fresh vegetables, she would make sure it had a bit more liquid than usual. In a separate cast iron pot with an enameled interior she would cook up the plain millet kasha. Once it was time to eat she would ladle the soup into large plates or bowls and everyone would place as much millet kasha in the middle as they wanted. We would make piping hot yellow millet islands in the middle of a hot orange-red ocean of borscht. For extra flavour some members of our family would put a little piece of hot red pepper into the borscht to give it a spicy kick. The aroma was magnificent and the taste was unforgettable.

At Breakfast by Zinaida Serebriakova, 1914. TRETYAKOV GALLERY, MOSCOW.

The painter depicted her own children waiting for breakfast. Made in 1914, this painting very clearly shows a stable middle class household—not too rich and not too poor. All children are well dressed, clean white linen covers the table and a soup tureen is in the main focus. The maid is ladelling out clear soup that looks like it could be consommé. The table is also set with a simple sugar bowl, some cookies, some fresh baked buns, a crystal carafe with water and a jar of milk. Note the little brown clay *gorshochek* at the plate of the boy who sits with his back to the painter. Most likely there is kasha inside as it is the most common break-fast food for children.

Smoked Bacon, Shallot and Millet Kasha,
top and bottom; Wild Mushroom and
Roasted Buckwheat Kasha, right (p. 114)

Smoked Bacon, Shallot and Millet Kasha

Pshennaja kasha s salom i lukom

1 Tbsp (15 mL) butter

¼ cup (60 mL) smoked bacon, cubed

4 small shallots, chopped

1 cup (250 mL) millet

2½ cups (625 mL) water or broth

¼ tsp (1 mL) salt

¼ tsp (1 mL) black pepper

This delicious and aromatic dish is great served on its own or as a side dish. Pork back fat can be used instead of bacon if desired.

In a small frying pan melt the butter; add bacon and shallots and sauté on medium-high heat until shallots are lightly browned. Set aside.

In a fine sieve, rinse millet under cold running water until water runs clear. Place millet in a saucepan, add the water or broth and cook on low heat until all liquid is absorbed and millet grains are tender, about 20 minutes. When ready, remove from heat and add the reserved shallot and bacon mixture, including the fat drippings, to the millet. Season with salt and pepper and stir well. Serve hot as a main dish or as a side.

MAKES 4 SERVINGS

PREPARATION TIME: 10 MINUTES

COOKING TIME: 20 MINUTES

Barley Kasha

Perlovaya kasha

1 cup (250 mL) pearl barley
2½ (625 mL) cups water
½ tsp (2 mL) salt
¼ cup (60 mL) butter

Serve this kasha on its own as a main course or as a side with meat. Pearl barley is the most popular type of barley used in Russian cooking.

In a sieve, rinse barley under cold running water until water runs clear. Place barley in a saucepan, add the water and cook on low heat until all liquid is absorbed and barley grains are tender, about 30 minutes. When ready, remove from heat, add salt and butter, and mix well. Serve hot.

MAKES 4 SERVINGS
PREPARATION TIME: 10 MINUTES
COOKING TIME: 30 MINUTES

NOTE: For a more tender texture, soak barley in cold water overnight. In the morning, drain the water, add 2 cups (500 mL) fresh water and cook on medium-low heat until all liquid is absorbed and barley grains are tender.

Butternut Squash and Rice Kasha

Risovaja kasha s tikvoy

1 small butternut squash
1 cup (250 mL) long grain white rice
2 cups (500 mL) milk
3 Tbsp butter
½ cup (125 mL) cream (35%)

This tender and delicate kasha can be served as a satisfying breakfast. You can also use other types of squash, such as acorn squash, to make this dish.

Pierce the whole washed squash with a fork in several places, place on a baking tray and bake at 400°F (200°C) for about 1 hour, until it can be easily sliced with a sharp knife. Cut the squash in half, remove the seeds and discard them. Spoon out 1 cup (250 mL) flesh and mash it. Save any remaining squash for future use.

In a sieve, rinse rice under cold running water until water runs clear. Place rice in a small saucepan, add milk and cook on medium heat until liquid is absorbed and rice is firm but cooked through, about 20 minutes. When ready, add mashed butternut squash, butter, cream and mix well. Transfer to a ceramic ovenproof dish and bake at 350°F (175°C) for 15 to 20 minutes. Serve hot.

MAKES 4 SERVINGS
PREPARATION TIME: 10 MINUTES
COOKING TIME: 1 HOUR 40 MINUTES

NOTE: Millet can be used in this recipe instead of rice.

Blini

LINIS (RUSSIAN CREPES) HAVE EXISTED for centuries virtually unchanged. Traditional Russian blinis have savoury or sweet fillings, and are especially popular during Maslenitsa—a holiday celebrated during the spring equinox that has its origins in pagan traditions. In the early days, the round shape of the blini symbolized the sun, and was associated with the Slavic sun god Yarilo. Maslenitsa was the time to celebrate the end of winter and the beginning of spring, before the onset of Lent. In a way, it was a very strategic holiday, which allowed people to use up delicious non-Lenten foods and ingredients before the fasting period.

Yeast-Leavened Russian Blini

Russkie blini na drozzhah

2 tsp (10 mL) yeast

2 cups (500 mL) warm milk

1 tsp (5 mL) salt

1 Tbsp (15 mL) sugar

2 eggs

1 Tbsp (15 mL) vegetable oil

2 cups (500 mL) all-purpose flour

In this recipe, you can mix the ingredients by hand or use a blender.

In a deep bowl, dissolve yeast in the warm milk by stirring lightly. Add salt, sugar, eggs, oil and flour and blend together to form a runny batter consistency. Let the batter rest in a warm place, such as the counter near the stove, for 1 to 1½ hours. Once the batter starts to rise, be careful not to leave it too long so that it runs and spills onto the counter.

Heat a well-greased frying pan over medium-high heat. Mix the batter with a large spoon, then pour or scoop the batter onto the pan, using approximately ¼ to ½ cup (60 to 125 mL) for each blini. Tilt the pan in a circular motion so that the batter coats the pan surface evenly. Fry each blini for about 2 minutes, until the bottom is golden. Loosen with a spatula, carefully flip over and cook the other side. Serve hot.

MAKES 8 SERVINGS

PREPARATION TIME: 1½ HOURS

COOKING TIME: 30 MINUTES

BLINI TOPPINGS AND SERVING SUGGESTIONS

Proper serving of Russian blini requires an abundance of small dishes for toppings, set on the main table, with the constant addition of stacks of freshly baked blini throughout the meal. It is not the type of meal that has a fixed serving per plate, but rather a continuous process of baking, serving, eating and drinking. Typical blini toppings include melted butter, fresh chopped scallions (they were often grown indoors on window sills), salmon, caviar, caramelized onions, sour cream, sugar, lemon juice, *varenye* and honey.

Buckwheat Blini

Grechnyevie blini

2 cups (500 mL) buckwheat flour

1 cup (250 mL) all-purpose flour

1 tsp (5 mL) salt

1 tsp (5 mL) sugar

3 Tbsp (45 mL) vegetable oil

4 cups (1 L) milk

2 eggs

½ cup (125 mL) melted butter

½ cup (125 mL) sour cream

This is an old Russian recipe that was forgotten for some time but now is returning to popularity. Russian blini are large and thin. You can roll them up or fold them into quarters before serving.

In a deep bowl, combine buckwheat flour, all-purpose flour, salt, sugar and vegetable oil. Gradually add the eggs and milk whisking constantly, to make a runny batter. Let the batter rest for about 15 minutes.

Heat a well-greased frying pan over medium-high heat. Mix the batter with a large spoon, then pour or scoop the batter onto the pan, using approximately ¼ to ½ cup (60 to 125 mL) for each blini. Tilt the pan in a circular motion so that the batter coats the pan surface evenly. Fry each blini for about 2 minutes, until the bottom is golden. Loosen with a spatula, carefully flip over and cook the other side. Serve hot.

Serve buckwheat blini with melted butter and sour cream.

MAKES 8 SERVINGS

PREPARATION TIME: 10 MINUTES

COOKING TIME: 20 MINUTES

Oat Blini

Ovsyannie blini

⅔ cup (160 mL) all-purpose flour

⅓ cup (80 mL) oat flour

1 tsp (5 mL) salt

1 Tbsp (15 mL) sugar

2 Tbsp (30 mL) vegetable oil

2 eggs

1½ cups (375 mL) warm milk

½ cup (125 mL) melted butter

½ cup (125 mL) honey

This type of blini has a very delicate flavour. It is a great option for a Sunday lunch.

In a deep bowl, combine all-purpose flour, oat flour, salt and sugar. While whisking gently, add vegetable oil, eggs and milk to make a runny batter. Let the batter rest for 10 to 15 minutes.

Heat a well-greased frying pan over medium-high heat. Mix the batter with a large spoon, then pour or scoop the batter onto the pan, using approximately ¼ to ½ cup (60 to 125 mL) for each blini. Tilt the pan in a circular motion so that the batter coats the pan surface evenly. Fry each blini for about 2 minutes, until the bottom is golden. Loosen with a spatula, carefully flip over and cook the other side.

Serve oat blini hot with melted butter and honey.

MAKES 8 SERVINGS

PREPARATION TIME: 10 MINUTES

COOKING TIME: 20 MINUTES

Smoked Salmon and Herb–Layered Blini *Pirog*

Blinchatij pirog s lososem

2 tsp (10 mL) yeast

2 cups (250 mL) warm milk

1 tsp (5 mL) salt

1 Tbsp (15 mL) sugar

2 eggs

1 Tbsp (15 mL) vegetable oil

2 cups (500 mL) all-purpose flour

FILLING

½ cup (125 mL) sour cream (30%)

5 Tbsp (75 mL) fresh chives, finely
chopped

¼ cup (60 mL) fresh dill, finely
chopped

10 oz (300 g) smoked salmon, thinly
sliced

3 lemon slices, thinly cut

3 sprigs of fresh dill

This dish is made with multiple layers of blini and filling. It can be served as a main dish or as a side.

In a deep bowl, dissolve yeast in warm milk. Add salt, sugar, eggs, oil and flour to form a semi-liquid consistency. Let the batter rest in a warm place for 1 to 1½ hours.

Heat a well-greased frying pan over medium-high heat. Mix the batter with a large spoon, then pour or scoop the batter onto the pan, using approximately ¼ to ½ cup (60 to 125 mL) for each blini. Tilt the pan in a circular motion so that the batter coats the pan surface evenly. Fry each blini for about 2 minutes, until the bottom is golden. Loosen with a spatula, carefully flip over and cook the other side. Stack finished blini on a plate and let cool to room temperature.

To make the filling combine sour cream, chives and dill in a small bowl and mix well. Cut the salmon into small, bite-sized pieces and place in a separate bowl.

Place a blini on a serving plate, spread with a thin layer of sour cream mixture and then add a thin layer of smoked salmon. Place another blini on top and continue adding layers of sour cream, smoked salmon and blini until all items are used up. Finish with a blini layer and decorate the top with lemon slices and fresh dill. You should get approximately 8 layers.

To serve, cut the stack like a cake and serve in wedges on individual plates.

MAKES 10 SERVINGS

PREPARATION TIME: 1 HOUR 40 MINUTES

COOKING TIME: 20 MINUTES

Pink Blini

Rozovie blini

½ cup (125 mL) raw beets, grated
1½ cups (375 mL) warm water
1 egg
½ tsp (2 mL) salt
1 tsp (5 mL) sugar
2 Tbsp (30 mL) butter
1 cup (250 mL) + 2 Tbsp (30 mL)
   flour

These blini were a favourite of the famous Russian poet Alexander Pushkin.

In a small bowl, cover grated beets with warm water and let stand for 20 to 30 minutes. Using a sieve to catch the grated beets, drain the water into a large mixing bowl (discard beets or save for another use). Add the egg, salt, sugar and melted butter to the bowl and whisk together with the water. Gradually add the flour to make a runny batter.

Heat a well-greased frying pan over medium-high heat. Mix the batter with a large spoon, then pour or scoop the batter onto the pan, using approximately ¼ to ½ cup (60 to 125 mL) for each blini. Tilt the pan in a circular motion so that the batter coats the pan surface evenly. Fry each blini for about 2 minutes, until the bottom is golden. Loosen with a spatula, carefully flip over and cook the other side. Serve hot.

MAKES 6 SERVINGS
PREPARATION TIME: 40 MINUTES
COOKING TIME: 20 MINUTES

Soured Milk Blini

Blini na prostokvashe

1 egg

2 Tbsp (30 mL) sugar

½ tsp (2 mL) salt

5 Tbsp (75 mL) canola oil

2½ cups (625 mL) *Prostokvasha*
  (see p. 170) or kefir

2½ cups (625 mL) all-purpose flour

½ tsp (2 mL) baking powder

This kind of blini can be served for breakfast. Soured milk gives them a nice tangy flavour.

In a bowl combine egg with sugar, salt, oil and prostokvasha. Gradually add flour and baking powder, whisking constantly, making sure there are no lumps.

Heat a well-greased frying pan over medium-high heat. Mix the batter with a large spoon, then pour or scoop the batter onto the pan, using approximately ¼ to ½ cup (60 to 125 mL) for each blini. Tilt the pan in a circular motion so that the batter coats the pan surface evenly. Fry each blini for about 2 minutes, until the bottom is golden. Loosen with a spatula, carefully flip over and cook the other side. Serve hot.

MAKES 6 SERVINGS

PREPARATION TIME: 10 MINUTES

COOKING TIME: 20 MINUTES

Pirogi

RUSSIAN CUISINE IS KNOWN for the abundance and variety of baked goods, collectively called *pirogi* (*pirog*, singular). One of the most distinct characteristics of *pirogi* is the use of dough as a wrapping medium for both savoury and sweet fillings. In North America, people are more familiar with *pirogi* as the adopted Eastern European name for boiled dumplings with potato and cheese filling; however, Russian *pirogi* have a much broader definition, encompassing savoury and sweet baked goods. Savoury *pirogi* are usually baked during holidays or for special occasions since they require more preparation time. They can be served as a main dish or as a side dish.

Russian *pirogi* come in a variety of shapes and sizes with a myriad of different fillings:

Pirozhki	Small, baked or fried oval buns with a filling; they can be held in hand and eaten as a convenient snack, or served as a side dish. They can be either sweet or savoury. Savoury fillings can be made from vegetables (carrots, beets or potatoes), mushrooms, fish, meat or kasha. *Varenye* is often used as a sweet filling for *pirozhki* as well as fruit, such as berries, apples or pears.
Rasstegai	Similar in shape to *pirozhki*, but with a hole at the top, allowing for the addition of fresh broth before serving. Traditionally, *rasstegai* were made with fillings that included fish, or a small slice of fish was placed in the hole.
Kurnik	A round, relatively large dome-shaped baked good with a thick layer of chicken filling. Sometimes, *kurniks* have multiple layers of different filling, separated by layers of blini (the Russian version of crepes).
Koulebyaka	One of the ancient baked goods, usually rectangular in shape, with complex savoury fillings that may include mushrooms, buckwheat kasha, fish (dried or boiled), hard-boiled eggs, onions and cabbage. The filling is either layered, or distributed so that each corner has its own filling. In some cases, when multiple fillings are used, blinis are used for separation. Often, *koulebyakas* were given the shape of their contents—fish shape for *koulebyaka* with salmon, mushroom shape for *koulebyaka* with porcini or chanterelle mushrooms.
Shangi	A variety of savoury open-faced *pirozhki* where filling is not wrapped in dough but spread on the top.
Sweet pirogi	These can be either closed (with a layer of dough on top) or with a lattice topping, exposing the sweet filling. Sweet *pirogi* are typically served for dessert as an accompaniment to tea. Apples, pears, plums, apricots and berries with sugar are usually used for filling.

Potato-Topped *Shangi*

Shangi s kartoshkoi

DOUGH

1 Tbsp (15 mL) yeast

¾ cup (185 mL) milk, divided

3 cups (750 mL) all-purpose
  flour, sifted

½ tsp (2 mL) salt

1 tsp (5 mL) sugar

7 Tbsp (105 mL) butter,
  divided

FILLING

¾ lb (375 g) potatoes, peeled

¼ cup (60 mL) butter, divided

¼ cup (60 mL) whipping
  cream (35%)

1 egg, beaten

Shangi (also known as *shanezhki*) are a variety of open-face *pirozhki*, originating from the Ural region. Recipes vary from one region to another, but *shangi* all have two characteristics in common: they have a round shape, and the filling is placed on top rather than folded into the dough as is done with common *pirozhki*. They can be made from sourdough or plain bread dough, with sweet or savoury fillings. My grandmother was an excellent *shangi* baker and this is her recipe.

In a small bowl, dissolve yeast in ¼ cup (60 mL) warm milk. In a separate bowl, combine sifted flour, salt, sugar and 1 Tbsp (15 mL) butter. Add yeast liquid and the rest of the milk, and mix together to form a smooth, soft dough. Cover with a clean tea towel and let the dough rise for about 1½ hours.

Prepare the filling by boiling the potatoes until tender, and then mash together with 1 Tbsp (15 mL) butter, whipping cream and a well-beaten egg.

Once the dough has rested, knead gently and shape into balls about the size of a plum. Flatten the dough balls into discs of about ½-inch (1 cm) thickness and place on a baking sheet. Make a small dent in the middle of each disc, and fill with the potato mixture. Melt 2 Tbsp (30 mL) butter and brush generously over the dough and surface of the potatoes surface. Let the *shangi* rest at room temperature for about 30 minutes.

Preheat oven to 400°F (200°C). Bake *shangi* about 20 minutes, or until golden. Remove from oven, brush again with the remaining 2 Tbsp (30 mL) melted butter and serve warm.

MAKES 10 SERVINGS

PREPARATION TIME: 1 HOUR 40 MINUTES

COOKING TIME: 20 MINUTES

NOTE: *Shangi* are the perfect food for travel. The filling bakes on well and does not smudge. They can be transported in glass or plastic boxes or simply wrapped in a clean tea towel.

Oat-Topped Rye *Musniki*

Rzhanie musniki s ovsyannoi nachinkoi

DOUGH

1 Tbsp (15 mL) yeast

¾ cup (185 mL) milk or water, divided

3 cups (750 mL) rye flour, sifted

½ tsp (2 mL) salt

1 tsp (5 mL) sugar

6 Tbsp (90 mL) butter, softened, divided

FILLING

1½ cups (375 mL) oat flour

¼ cup (60 mL) water

1 tsp (5 mL) salt

2 Tbsp (30 mL) butter, divided

These *musniki* (singular: *musnik*) are a variety of *shangi*, a specialty of the Vyatka region. What makes them special is that the filling is made from a different kind of dough. This is my grandmother's recipe.

In a small bowl, dissolve yeast in ¼ cup (60 mL) warm milk or water. In a separate bowl combine sifted flour, salt, sugar and 2 Tbsp (30 mL) butter. Add yeast liquid and the rest of the milk and mix together to form a smooth, soft dough. Cover with a clean tea towel and let the dough rise for about 1½ hours.

Prepare the dough filling by mixing together the oat flour, water, salt and 2 Tbsp (30 mL) butter.

Once dough has rested, knead gently and shape into balls about the size of a plum. Flatten the dough balls into discs of about ½-inch (1 cm) thickness and place on a baking sheet. Make a small dent in the middle of each disc and place a little bit of oat dough filling in each. Generously brush with 2 Tbsp (30 mL) melted butter and let them rest for about 30 minutes.

Preheat oven to 400°F (200°C). Bake *musniki* for about 20 minutes, or until golden. Remove from oven, brush them again with the remaining 2 Tbsp (30 mL) melted butter and serve warm.

MAKES 10 SERVINGS

PREPARATION TIME: 2 HOURS 20 MINUTES

COOKING TIME: 20 MINUTES

Kalachi

— ❧ —

1½ cups (375 mL) milk, lukewarm

6 eggs + 1 beaten egg white, divided

2 tsp (10 mL) yeast

3 cups (750 mL) all-purpose flour

3 Tbsp (45 mL) sugar

3 Tbsp (45 mL) softened butter +
  3 Tbsp (45 mL) melted butter,
  divided

1 tsp (5 mL) salt

Kalach (plural: *kalachi*) is a type of Russian street food. It is usually purchased at a bakery and eaten outdoors. The bun resembles the shape of a lock and has a special handle, which makes it easy to hold. Typically, only the bun part is eaten and handle is discarded.

In a mixing bowl, combine milk, 6 eggs, yeast and flour. Cover bowl with clean tea towel and let it stand in a warm place for 40 to 60 minutes until the dough rises quite a bit and then falls.

Once the dough falls, add sugar, softened butter and salt and knead well. Cover the dough with clean tea towel and let it rest for an additional 20 to 30 minutes.

Divide the dough into seven equal pieces. With a rolling pin roll six pieces into flat rounds about ¾ inch (2 cm) thick. Roll the last portion of dough into a long log about ¾ inch (2 cm) in diameter and cut into six equal pieces—these will be the handles for the *kalachi*.

Brush each dough round with the melted butter, fold in half and attach the handle on both ends of the fold. Generously glaze *kalachi* with beaten egg white. Place on a baking sheet and put in 350°F (175°C) oven for about 15 to 20 minutes, or until golden brown and a toothpick inserted in the thickest part comes out clean.

MAKES 6 SERVINGS
PREPARATION TIME: 2 HOURS 30 MINUTES
COOKING TIME: 30 MINUTES

OPPOSITE PAGE: *Baker* by Boris Kustodiev, 1920. I.I. BRODSKY APARTMENT-MUSEUM.

A cheerful gentleman with a fashionable moustache is placing a little éclair in a box full of pastries. His shop is full of wonderful typical baked goods loved by many Russians. On the right and left in rich garlands are the baranki—dry ring shaped cookies sold on a string. They make a great accompaniment to tea. Behind the baker we can see a row of white French loaves and darker rye bread on the shelf below. On the counter you can see some fresh *kalachi* on the left and a pile of assorted buns, crescents covered with poppy seeds and some fine pastries behind the glass display. These are all items Russian people would typically go to a bakery shop to buy.

Apple *Pirozhki*

Pirozhki s yablokami

DOUGH

2 tsp (10 mL) yeast

1 cup (250 mL) milk or water at
    room temperature

2 Tbsp (30 mL) sugar

1 tsp (5 mL) salt

1 egg

2 cups (500 mL) + 2 Tbsp (30 mL)
    all-purpose flour, divided

2 Tbsp (30 mL) butter, softened

1 tsp (5 mL) vegetable oil

1 egg white, beaten

FILLING

3 medium-size tart apples, peeled,
    cored and finely diced

¼ cup (60 mL) sugar (approx.)

This is one of the most popular types of sweet pirozhki. You can try different kinds of apple varieties for the filling. Most often sweet pirozhki are served with tea as a snack.

In a deep bowl dissolve yeast in warm milk; add sugar, salt and egg and mix well. Gradually add 2 cups (500 mL) flour and the butter, and knead the dough until it stops sticking to fingers. Cover dough with a clean tea towel and put in a warm place such as the counter near the oven to rise for 40 minutes.

Knead the dough well again to let the gas bubbles escape. Brush with vegetable oil, cover with tea towel, and let rise for another 30 to 40 minutes.

On a clean working surface dusted with 2 Tbsp (30 mL) flour, roll the dough into about a ½-inch (1 cm) thick sheet. Use a cookie cutter or a drinking glass to cut out rounds. Put 1 Tbsp (15 mL) diced apples and 1 tsp (5 mL) sugar in the middle of each round, fold the ends together and seal well, giving the *pirozhki* a round or oblong shape; place on a baking sheet with the seal facing down. Let the *pirozhki* rest on the baking sheet for 15 to 20 minutes.

Preheat oven to 350°F (175°C). Glaze *pirozhki* with beaten egg white and bake in preheated oven for about 30 minutes, until golden brown. Serve warm.

MAKES 10 SERVINGS

PREPARATION TIME: 2 HOURS 30 MINUTES

COOKING TIME: 30 MINUTES

NOTE: Do not premix apples and sugar, as sugar will draw out apple juices making it impossible to seal *pirozhki* properly. To avoid leakage, you can add ¼ tsp (1 mL) flour on top of raw apples while arranging them on the dough. Extra flour will bind the sweet syrup and prevent leakage.

NOTE: You can also use other fruits such as blueberries or apricots as fillings in sweet *pirozki*.

Cabbage Pie

Pirog s kapustoi

This is a classic Russian *pirog.* You can also add chopped hardboiled eggs to the filling. *Schi,* kasha, a large mug of *kvas* and this particular *pirog* make a very typical traditional Russian meal.

DOUGH

2 tsp (10 mL) yeast

1 cup (250 mL) milk or water at room temperature

2 Tbsp (30 mL) sugar

1 tsp (5 ml) salt

1 egg

3 cups (750 mL) all-purpose flour

2 Tbsp (30 mL) butter or vegetable oil

FILLING

¼ cup (60 mL) butter

3 large shallots, chopped

½ small head of white cabbage, finely shredded

¼ cup (60 mL) chicken, vegetable or mushroom broth

½ tsp (2 mL) salt

1 tsp (5 mL) black pepper

GLAZE

3 Tbsp (45 mL) vegetable oil or 1 egg white, lightly beaten

NOTE: You can also mold the *pirog* into a circle shape, as well as adding decorative dough designs to the top. If using decorations, make sure you brush them with the glaze

DOUGH

In a deep bowl, dissolve yeast in warm milk; add sugar, salt and egg and mix well. Gradually add flour and butter, and knead the dough until it stops sticking to fingers. Cover dough with a clean tea towel and put in a warm place to let rise for 1 hour. Then, knead again to let the gas bubbles escape, cover with the tea towel, and let rise for another 30 to 40 minutes.

FILLING

In a deep skillet, melt the butter and add the shallots. Mix well and set on medium heat. Add cabbage and broth and sauté, covered, for 15 to 20 minutes, stirring occasionally. Once cabbage is limp, add salt and pepper. Remove the lid to let excess water evaporate and continue sautéing until cabbage is tender. Set aside, and cool to room temperature.

ASSEMBLY

Dust a clean, non-stick surface with a bit of flour and roll the dough to about ½-inch (1 cm) thickness. Transfer the dough to a non-stick baking sheet. Place the cabbage filling on one half of the dough; drape the other half of the dough over the filling and seal tightly at the seams making a square shape. With a fork, pierce the top in several places to let steam escape. Let the *pirog* sit for about 20 minutes at room temperature.

Preheat oven to 350°F (175°C) and brush the top of the *pirog* with vegetable oil or beaten egg white. Bake for 30 to 40 minutes until golden brown. Serve warm.

MAKES 10 SERVINGS

PREPARATION TIME: 2 HOURS

COOKING TIME: 30 MINUTES

Salmon-Filled *Rasstegai*

Rasstegai s semgoy

Rasstegai are savoury boat-shaped *pirogi* with an elegant opening on top, exposing the filling. Typically they are served as a side with soup.

DOUGH

DOUGH

2 tsp (10 mL) yeast

1 cup (250 mL) milk or water at
   room temperature

2 Tbsp (30 mL) sugar

1 tsp (5 mL) salt

1 egg

2 cups (500 mL) all-purpose flour

2 Tbsp (30 mL) butter or vegetable
   oil

In a deep bowl, dissolve yeast in warm milk; add sugar, salt and egg and mix well. Gradually add flour and butter, and knead the dough until it stops sticking to fingers. Cover dough with a clean tea towel and put in a warm place to let rise for 1 hour. Then, knead it again to let the gas bubbles escape, cover with the tea towel, and let rise for another 30 to 40 minutes.

FILLING

FILLING

2 onions, diced

¼ cup (60 mL) butter or vegetable
   oil

½ lb (250 g) salmon fillets, boiled
   and diced

1 tsp (5 mL) salt

1 tsp (5 mL) black pepper

1 cup (250 mL) fish broth (approx.)

Sauté the diced onions in butter until lightly golden, about 10 minutes. Add diced salmon fillets, season with salt and pepper and mix well. Sauté until the salmon is seared on all sides.

GLAZE

ASSEMBLY

1 egg white, beaten

3 Tbsp (45 mL) melted butter

Divide the dough into ten small portions, rolling each into ½ inch (1 cm) thick rounds, approximately the size of a saucer. Place about 2 to 3 Tbsp (30 to 45 mL) filling in the middle of each dough round. Bring the edges together and seal (leave a ¾-inch (2 cm) opening in the middle) making the *rasstegai* boat shape. Place *rasstegai* on a well-greased baking sheet and let them rest for 20 to 30 minutes.

Preheat oven to 400°F (200°C). Glaze *rasstegai* with beaten egg white, and bake in oven for about 15 minutes, until golden brown. Remove from oven, glaze with melted butter and pour 1 to 2 Tbsp (15 to 30 mL) fish broth into each of the openings. Serve hot.

MAKES 10 SERVINGS

PREPARATION TIME: 2 HOURS 30 MINUTES

COOKING TIME: 30 MINUTES

Salmon, Rice and Egg *Koulebyaka*

Klassicheskaya koulebyaka s lososem risom i yaycami

DOUGH

2 tsp (10 mL) yeast

1 cup (250 mL) milk or water at
room temperature

2 Tbsp (30 mL) sugar

1 tsp (5 mL) salt

1 egg

2 cups (500 mL) all-purpose flour

2 Tbsp (30 mL) butter or vegetable
oil

RICE STUFFING

½ cup (125 mL) long-grain white rice

¼ cup (60 mL) vegetable oil

1 medium onion, diced

1 tsp (5 mL) salt

SALMON STUFFING

0.9 lb (400 g) salmon fillets or
1 can flaked salmon

½ bunch fresh dill, chopped

1 tsp (5 mL) black pepper

EGG STUFFING

4 large hard-boiled eggs, peeled
and finely chopped

1 tsp (5 mL) salt

1 tsp (5 mL) black pepper

2 Tbsp (30 mL) butter, melted

GLAZE

1 egg, beaten

3 Tbsp (45 mL) butter, divided

This is the most well-known, classic version of *koulebyaka*. It was made at home and also served in restaurants and *traktir* (eateries).

DOUGH

In a deep bowl, dissolve yeast in warm milk; add sugar, salt and egg and mix well. Gradually add flour and butter, and knead the dough until it stops sticking to fingers. Cover dough with clean tea towel and put in a warm place to let rise for 1 hour. Then, knead it again to let the gas bubbles escape, cover with tea towel, and let rise for another 30 to 40 minutes.

RICE STUFFING

Place the rice in a saucepan, cover with 1 cup (250 mL) water and cook on medium heat until al dente. Drain excess water. In a frying pan, heat oil, add onion and salt, and sauté until the onion is golden brown, about 5 minutes. Transfer the onion to the saucepan with the rice and mix well. Set aside.

SALMON STUFFING

If using fillets, place them in boiling water and cook for about 5 minutes, until they are cooked though. Drain the water, finely chop the fillet and place pieces in a bowl. Add chopped fresh dill and ground pepper; mix well and set aside. (If using canned salmon, simply mix with the dill and pepper.)

EGG STUFFING

Place finely chopped eggs in bowl. Season with salt and pepper, mix with melted butter and set aside.

ASSEMBLY

Roll the dough into a ½-inch (1 cm) thick rectangle and carefully place it on a well-greased baking sheet. On half the surface, evenly spread the rice stuffing, leaving about ¾ inch (2 cm) free around the edges. In the same manner, spread the salmon stuffing on top of the rice stuffing, followed by the egg stuffing. Carefully fold the free half of the dough rectangle over the stuffing, and seal the seams around the perimeter. Let the *koulebyaka* sit at room temperature for about 15 to 20 minutes

To glaze, mix together the beaten egg and 2 Tbsp (30 mL) melted butter, and use this mixture to glaze the top of the *koulebyaka*. With a fork, pierce the top dough layer in several places to let steam escape. Bake at 400°F (200°C) until dough is baked through and golden brown, about 40 to 50 minutes. Remove from oven, glaze with remaining melted butter and let sit for 2 to 3 minutes. Serve warm.

MAKES 6 SERVINGS
PREPARATION TIME: 2 HOURS 30 MINUTES
COOKING TIME: 30 MINUTES

NOTE: With a little bit of creativity you can use some extra dough to make decorative leaves, flowers, mushrooms, etc. You might also decorate or shape the *koulebyaka* to match the filling. For example, if using a salmon filling, shape the *koulebyaka* into a fish, or use dough to make fish decorations. Apply all decorations before glazing the *koulebyaka* with beaten egg and butter.

Kurnik

DOUGH

2 tsp (10 mL) yeast

1⅓ cups (330 mL) milk or water at
   room temperature

2 Tbsp (30 mL) sugar

1 tsp (5 mL) salt

1 egg

2 cups (500 mL) all-purpose flour

2 Tbsp (30 mL) butter (or vegetable
   oil)

RICE FILLING

1 cup (250 mL) arborio rice

1 Tbsp (15 mL) vegetable oil

1 medium onion, diced

½ tsp (2 mL) salt

MUSHROOM FILLING

2 Tbsp (30 mL) butter

2 cups (500 mL) fresh mushrooms,
   thinly sliced

2 Tbsp (30 mL) fresh dill, chopped

CHICKEN AND EGG FILLING

1 medium chicken (about 3 lb
   [1.5 kg])

½ bunch fresh parsley

5 eggs, hardboiled and diced

GLAZE

1 egg

3 Tbsp (45 mL) butter, melted

This is a dome shaped *pirog* with three different fillings: rice, mushroom and a chicken and egg mixture. It was usually prepared for big occasions such as weddings and served along with some chicken broth on the side.

DOUGH

In a deep bowl, dissolve yeast in warm milk; add sugar, salt and egg and mix well. Gradually add flour and butter, and knead the dough until it stops sticking to fingers. Cover dough with a clean tea towel and put in a warm place to let rise for 1 hour. Then, knead it again to let the gas bubbles escape, cover with the tea towel, and let rise for another 30 to 40 minutes.

RICE FILLING

Place the rice in a saucepan, cover with 2 cups (500 mL) water and cook on medium heat until done, about 20 minutes. Drain excess water. In a frying pan, heat oil, add onion and salt, and sauté until the onion is golden brown, about 5 minutes. Transfer the onion to the saucepan with the rice and mix well. Set aside.

MUSHROOM FILLING

In a frying pan, heat the butter; add the mushrooms and sauté until tender, about 5 to 10 minutes. Add dill and mix well.

CHICKEN AND EGG FILLING

Wash the chicken, trim excess fat and place in a deep saucepan. Cover with water, add parsley and simmer on medium-low heat for about 1 hour until chicken is tender and cooked through. Set the chicken broth aside. Remove the skin and bones from the chicken and mince all the meat finely, placing it in a bowl. Add the diced eggs and combine.

(CONTINUED NEXT PAGE)

Kurnik (continued)

ASSEMBLY

Divide the dough into two pieces—a slightly larger one for the top cover of the *kurnik*, and a smaller one for the bottom. Roll the smaller piece of dough into a circle about ⅝ inch (1.5 cm) thick and big enough to fit in a round, deep, well-greased metal or glass pie pan about 8 inches (20 cm) in diameter. The dough should cover the entire bottom and walls of the pan, hanging off the sides about ¼ inch (6 mm). Place rice stuffing in the center of the dough lined pan, forming a dome shape. Compress it gently so that there is a gradual tapering to the edge of the pan, with more filling in the middle. Use the same technique for the mushroom filling and then the chicken and egg filling, layering them on top of the rice.

Preheat oven to 350°F (175°C). Roll the second piece of dough into a larger circle; cover the filling with it and firmly seal the top and bottom edges together. At the top of the *kurnik*, use a knife to make an opening that lets steam escape during baking. Glaze the dough surface with beaten egg and bake for about 1 hour. *Kurnik* is ready when steam comes out of the center opening and bottom dough layer is thoroughly cooked. Serve hot with some chicken broth on the side.

Makes 6 servings
Preparation time: 2 hours 30 minutes
Cooking time: 30 minutes

NOTE: For a special touch, you can decorate the surface of the *kurnik* with cut out dough ornaments and bake as indicated. See page 141 for ideas how to decorate with dough ornaments.

MY MOTHER'S MEMOIR: *Mushroom Picking*

We once went to our friend's dacha (summer house) in order to pick some chanterelles in the nearby forest. We left early in the morning and decided to go deep in the woods in the hope of finding more mushrooms there. Once you go looking for one particular kind of mushroom all other mushrooms are no longer noticeable. The thrill and joy of a mushroom hunt is similar to the thrill you get when you catch a big fish or find a treasure. Most people who go mushroom picking have their favourite spots where they know mushrooms grow every year. So we checked all our secret spots, but alas, no chanterelles anywhere! Tired and a bit disappointed, we sat down on a log to have some tea from our thermos before heading back. Suddenly I noticed a little mound under the fallen leaves. It was a tiny "butter mushroom" peeking from the ground! Butter mushrooms, or as they are called in Russian "maslyata," are a type of edible mushroom named for its shiny cap that looks like it's been glazed with butter. The joy of this discovery was understandable—these mushrooms grow in group, so if you find one there are surely more somewhere around. So within 15 minutes we picked full baskets of butter mushrooms instead of chanterelles, right where we were walking earlier that morning, hoping to find chanterelles but not noticing anything else. Once we came back to the dacha we pan fried the mushrooms with some young potatoes, onions and fresh dill. This was the true aroma of the summer!

Desserts and Beverages

RADITIONAL RUSSIAN SWEETS required minimal processing and were primarily eaten as is. Typical children's treats were apples, nuts, honey, berries and other seasonal fruits. During the periods when certain fruits and berries were abundant other desserts were prepared that required more ingredients and attention such as *pastila* (soft fruit candy), marmalade (very different from the British version) and fruit *kisels* (soft jelly-filled desserts).

The staple traditional Russian beverage was *kvas*. It has been around since ancient times and is still very popular today. It is made from rye bread fermented in water. Other typical drinks like non-alcoholic fruit-infused waters were made as refreshments, and many households had their own specialty drink. Wine was mostly imported due to cold winters, and beer was produced locally, but not in large amounts. Tea was always the non-alcoholic drink of choice; however coffee was also consumed on a smaller scale.

Rowan Berry *Pastila*

Ryabinovaya pastila

4 cups (1 L) fresh rowan berries

2 cups (500 mL) sugar

4 cups (1 L) water

1 cup (250 mL) powdered sugar

This type of soft fruit candy was a popular treat among kids. It is very similar to modern fruit leather–type sweets.

Put freshly picked rowan berries in the freezer for at least 24 hours to remove bitterness. Place frozen berries on a baking sheet and bake in 210°F (100°C) oven for about 2 hours, until berries are softened.

While berries are baking, heat the water in a medium saucepan with the sugar and stir constantly until sugar completely dissolves and liquid covers back of the spoon in a consistency similar to liquid honey.

Remove berries from oven. Strain the berries right away through a fine sieve to remove skins and seeds, collecting the puree in a large sauce pan. While the puree is still hot, add thick sugar syrup. Continue heating the purée on medium-low heat, whisking frequently for about an hour so the extra moisture evaporates and the purée thickens.

Line a baking sheet with parchment paper and pour the thickened purée onto the sheet. It will be thick and sticky so use a metal spoon to help spread it on the sheet. Bake at 160°F (70°C) for 1 to 1½ hours, until the *pastila* solidifies enough to be cut. Remove from the oven and cool on wire rack. Cut into bite-sized pieces, and dust with powdered sugar. Store in an airtight container at room temperature.

MAKES 6 SERVINGS

PREPARATION TIME: 30 MINUTES

COOKING TIME: 2 HOURS FOR BERRIES + 1½ HOURS FOR PASTILA

ROWAN BERRIES

The rowan berry is a bright orange berry that turns red in the winter. It is particularly hardy and can survive long winters. In fact, cold plays an important role in its growth—after the first real frost, bitter orange berries turn sweet and red. That is when rowan berries are harvested.

Apple *Pastila*

Yablochnaya pastila

———— ❦ ————

4 large tart apples
¼ cup (60 mL) honey
1 cup (250 mL) powdered sugar

This is a classic treat loved by all Russian kids. Although now most *pastila* is store-bought, in the past it was made at home. Somewhat similar in texture and flavour to fruit leather this great sweet snack was often served as an accompaniment to tea.

Place the apples in a baking dish and bake whole, uncovered at 350°F (175°C) for about an hour. Remove the apples from the oven and let them cool enough to be handled. Cut them open and scoop out the flesh, removing the seeds from inside and discarding them and the apple skins. Puree the apple flesh in a blender or food processor then transfer into a deep bowl. Add honey and beat with a handheld mixer for about 15 minutes until the puree becomes light beige in colour.

Transfer the whipped apple puree onto a baking sheet, lined with parchment paper and spread out into a layer about ¾ inch (2 cm) thick. Dry out the apple puree at 180°F (80°C) for about 6 hours. You should be able to peel the apple layer from the paper in a single piece once it is dried. Once the *pastila* had dried sufficiently, remove the tray from the oven and fold the *pastila* in half and then again in half, and again until you get a relatively thick block. Rub the powdered sugar on the sides of the *pastila* block and cut into bite-sized pieces. Rub all sides of each piece in powdered sugar so they are less sticky. Store in an airtight container at room temperature.

MAKES 6 SERVINGS
PREPARATION TIME: 40 MINUTES
COOKING TIME: 1 HOUR FOR APPLES + 6 HOURS FOR PASTILA

Gourievskaya Kasha

Gurievskaya kasha

1⁄3 cup (80 mL) hazelnuts, skin removed

1⁄3 cup (80 mL) walnuts

1⁄3 cup (80 mL) almonds, skin removed

5 Tbsp (75 mL) warm water

6 cups (1 1⁄2 L) coffee cream (18%)

1⁄2 cup (125 mL) Cream of Wheat

1⁄2 cup (125 mL) sugar

3 drops almond extract

1⁄2 tsp (2 mL) lemon zest

1⁄2 tsp (2 mL) ground cardamom

2 Tbsp (30 mL) butter

1⁄2 cup (125 mL) Cherry *Varenye* (from pitted cherries) (see p. 159) or cherry syrup

This baked Cream of Wheat dish was a very popular dessert dish at the end of 19th century. Today it is a recipe that people are curious about and that is well known, but rarely made. It can be made with coffee cream or with almond milk. Almond milk was widely used in Russian cuisine during Lent. It was used as a direct replacement for milk and cream in all recipes.

Preheat oven to 210°F (100°C).

Place the nuts and warm water in a food processor. Finely grind the nuts and set aside.

Pour the coffee cream into a wide, flat ovenproof dish and place in oven. Heat the cream, making sure that it doesn't boil, and gently remove the top layer of thickened cream with a wide, thin spatula or a broad knife once it starts to solidify. Reserve the thickened layer in a separate dish. Repeat the process using the same cream until 10 to 12 layers of thickened cream are collected. This should take about 15 to 20 minutes.

In a large saucepan, cook Cream of Wheat in the remaining cream until thoroughly cooked. Add sugar, half of the ground nuts, almond extract, lemon zest and cardamom and mix well.

Adjust heat of the oven to 350°F (175°C).

Butter a deep, ovenproof ceramic dish about 8 inches (20 cm) in diameter, and pour in about a third of the prepared Cream of Wheat (this should make about a 1⁄2-inch [1 cm] thick layer). Cover with half of the reserved thickened cream. Add another third of the Cream of Wheat followed by the remaining thickened cream. Add the last layer of Cream of Wheat and drizzle the top with about half the cherry *varenye*. Place in preheated oven and bake for 15 to 20 minutes.

Remove the kasha from the oven; decorate with the remaining *varenye*. Serve directly from the baking dish.

MAKES 4 SERVINGS

PREPARATION TIME: 40 MINUTES

COOKING TIME: 40 MINUTES

Cranberry *Kisel*, top left (p. 161);
Vatroushka, top right (p. 151);
Hvorost, bottom (p. 155)

Vatroushka

DOUGH

1½ cups (375 mL) all-purpose flour

¼ cup (60 mL) sour cream

2½ tsp (12 mL) yeast

2 egg yolks

½ cup (125 mL) butter, softened

½ tsp (2 mL) salt

1 tsp (5 mL) sugar

FILLING

2½ cups (625 mL) *Tvorog*
   (see p. 166) or pressed unsalted
   cottage cheese

3 egg yolks

½ cup (125 mL) butter, softened

1 tsp (5 mL) vanilla extract

½ tsp (2 mL) salt

2 Tbsp (30 mL) sugar

1 tsp (5 mL) all-purpose flour

GLAZE

1 egg yolk, beaten

Vatroushka is similar in shape to a Danish and the filling has the consistency of cheesecake. The pastry is made with sourdough. You can add different berries to the filling to make blueberry, raspberry or cranberry *vatroushka*. It can also be made in different sizes, from two-bite-sized to the size of a dinner plate, which is cut up like a pie.

DOUGH

Place the flour on a clean work surface and make a well in the middle. In a small bowl, combine sour cream, yeast and egg yolks, and pour into the flour well. Gradually combine the wet mixture with about one-third of the flour, then add butter, salt and sugar and mix with the rest of the flour. Knead until dough is soft and does not stick to fingers. Place the dough into a bowl, cover with a tea towel and let it rest in a warm place, allowing dough to rise for about 45 minutes. Knead gently again, and let the dough rise under a clean tea towel for about 30 minutes.

FILLING

Drain extra liquid from the *tvorog* then press it through a sieve to make it as dry as possible. Discard the liquid and retain the white *tvorog* mass. In a bowl, combine the *tvorog* with egg yolks, butter, vanilla, salt, sugar and flour. Blend the mixture well until it becomes smooth.

ASSEMBLY

Preheat oven to 360°F (180°C). Roll the dough to a ¾-inch (2 cm) thickness and cut out six circles with a 4-inch (10 cm) diameter cookie cutter or drinking glass. Place about 2 Tbsp (30 mL) filling in the middle, leaving a wide dough rim. Glaze the dough rims with beaten egg yolk and use a fork to pierce the middle of *vatroushka*, where the filling is located in a few places. Place *vatroushkas* on a greased and floured baking tray. Bake for about 40 minutes until *vatroushkas* are light golden brown and slide easily off the baking sheet

MAKES 6 SERVINGS

PREPARATION TIME: 1 HOUR 40 MINUTES

COOKING TIME: 40 MINUTES

Russian Vanilla Gingerbread

Vanilnyi pryanik

⅓ cup (80 mL) unsalted butter

½ cup (125 mL) + 2 Tbsp (30 mL) honey

⅓ cup (80 mL) + 4 tsp (20 mL) milk

2 cups (500 mL) all-purpose flour (approx.), divided

2 Tbsp (30 mL) baking powder

1 Tbsp (15 mL) Gingerbread Spice (see below)

1 Tbsp (15 mL) vegetable oil

GLAZE

½ cup (125 mL) water

1 cup (250 mL) sugar

½ tsp (2 mL) vanilla extract

This typical Russian sweet treat can be made as small cookies or as a larger cake that is glazed and cut into individual portions.

Preheat oven to 325°F (160°C).

In a saucepan, melt the butter and gradually stir in all honey and milk. In a mixing bowl, combine 1⅔ cups (420 mL) flour, baking powder and Gingerbread Spice. Carefully pour the contents of the saucepan into the bowl with the flour and mix well to form a smooth dough. Grease square or round pie forms (about 7 inches [18 cm] in diameter) with vegetable oil. Lightly flour surface using reserved flour. You can use special forms for baking gingerbreads if desired. Transfer the gingerbread dough into the baking forms and bake for about 30 minutes until a toothpick inserted in the middle comes out clean.

To prepare the glaze, combine water and sugar in a small saucepan and heat, stirring constantly to make a transparent syrup. Once the sugar is completely dissolved and the syrup begins to boil with large bubbles (temperature should be around 225°F [105°C]), remove the saucepan from the heat and stir in vanilla extract. Cool down until it feels hot to touch but not scalding.

For large *pryanik* apply glaze on the entire surface with a pastry brush. If you are using smaller gingerbread forms remove the *pryaniks* from baking forms and dip into the syrup. Rest *pryaniks* on wire rack and let the glaze solidify.

MAKES 6 SERVINGS

PREPARATION TIME: 30 MINUTES

COOKING TIME: 30 MINUTES

Gingerbread Spice

10 Tbsp (150 mL) ground cinnamon

2 Tbsp (30 mL) ground cloves

2 Tbsp (30 mL) ground allspice

2 tsp (10 mL) black pepper

2 tsp (10 mL) ground cardamom

4 tsp (20 mL) ground ginger

Mix all spices together in a bowl. Spices can be used immediately or stored indefinitely in a sealed container.

MAKES 1 CUP (250 ML)

PREPARATION TIME: 10 MINUTES

Hvorost

½ cup (125 mL) milk

1 Tbsp (15 mL) sour cream (30%)

3 egg yolks

1 Tbsp (15 mL) sugar

¼ tsp (1 mL) salt

2 Tbsp (30 mL) brandy (or vodka)

2½ cups (625 mL) all-purpose flour

2 cups (500 mL) canola oil

½ cup (125 mL) powdered sugar

These deep-fried pastries are a traditional dish during Christmas holidays.

In a bowl combine milk, sour cream, egg yolks, sugar, salt and brandy. While mixing vigorously, gradually add flour to make a thick dough.

Roll out the dough to a very thin sheet ⅛ to ¼ inch (3 to 6 mm). Cut out long, thin strips of dough about 1¼ inches (3 cm) wide and then further cut these into 2-inch (5 cm) segments. In the middle of each piece, cut a small lengthwise slash and slip one of the ends through the slash, forming a twist.

In a deep skillet, heat oil and deep fry the dough twists one at a time. The twists should be able to swim freely in oil and cook through on all sides. After about 3 to 5 minutes when the *hvorost* becomes lightly golden, remove it with a slotted spoon and place finished *hvorost* on a plate, lined with a paper towel, to remove excess oil. Transfer the *hvorost* on a serving plate, dust with powdered sugar and serve warm or cold.

MAKES 10 SERVINGS

PREPARATION TIME: 30 MINUTES

COOKING TIME: 30 MINUTES

Almond *Blancmange* with Lingonberry Sauce

Blanmanzhe s brusničnim sousom

1 Tbsp (15 mL) gelatin

3 Tbsp (45 mL) warm water

⅓ cup (80 mL) almonds,
unblanched

2 cups (500 mL) milk

⅔ cup (160 mL) powdered sugar

3 Tbsp (45 mL) + 12 fresh or frozen
lingonberries, divided

3 Tbsp (45 mL) sugar

This is another typical 19th century dessert. Almonds were used frequently during Lent, and almond milk was often used instead of cow's milk in cooking. Lingonberries are abundant in Northern parts of Canada, but if you cannot find them you can substitute them with cranberries.

Presoak the gelatin in warm water and set aside.

Place the almonds in a small bowl, pour boiling water over them (enough to cover all almonds) and cover the bowl with a plate for a few minutes. Remove the plate and let the almonds rest in the water for 15 to 20 minutes.

Drain the water and remove the almond skins. Using a mortar or a food processor, grind the almonds into a paste while gradually adding all the milk.

Filter the mixture through a fine sieve or muslin cloth and squeeze as much liquid from the solid part as possible. Place the almond milk in a small saucepan and add powdered sugar. Carefully heat milk until it is almost boiling. As soon as small bubbles appear, add gelatin to the almond milk. Whisk vigorously until gelatin completely dissolves. Remove from heat.

Filter again, through a fine sieve or muslin and pour into 4 forms or serving cups about ½ cup (125 mL) each in volume. Chill in the refrigerator until *blancmange* completely solidifies, at least 2 hours.

To prepare the sauce, combine 3 Tbsp (45 mL) lingonberries and sugar in a small saucepan and heat on medium, stirring occasionally, until berries are tender and juices flow. Cool to room temperature.

Remove chilled *blancmange* from forms, arrange on individual dessert plates and garnish with lingonberry sauce and some berries.

MAKES 4 SERVINGS
PREPARATION TIME: 1 HOUR
COOKING TIME: 2 HOURS TO CHILL

Tvorog with Sour Cream

Tvorog so smetanoi

1 cup (250 mL) *Tvorog* (see p. 166) or pressed unsalted cottage cheese

½ cup (125 mL) sour cream (30%)

1 Tbsp (15 mL) Vanilla Sugar (see below)

¼ cup (60 mL) raisins

½ cup (125 mL) fresh berries (optional)

The combination of *tvorog* and sour cream makes this an excellent healthy breakfast. In summer, serve with fresh berries on the side.

In a ceramic or glass bowl combine *tvorog*, sour cream, sugar and raisins and mix well. Chill for about 20 minutes, allowing raisins to swell, then spoon into individual serving dishes. Garnish with fresh berries.

MAKES 4 SERVINGS
PREPARATION TIME: 10 MINUTES
COOKING TIME: 20 MINUTES TO CHILL

VANILLA SUGAR

You can make your own vanilla sugar by placing some regular granulated sugar in a glass jar with a tight seal and inserting one or several whole vanilla beans inside the jar. Keep the sugar tightly sealed and in about 2 weeks you will have a nicely perfumed supply of sugar for all your cooking needs. Retain the vanilla beans in the jar and replenish the sugar once in a while. Try using vanilla sugar in your baking, on top of breakfast cereal or in your coffee or tea.

Paskha

———— ❧ ————

This molded *tvorog* (cottage cheese) dish is a delectable ancient dessert that was served only on Easter. Traditionally, the *paskha* was always decorated with the letters X. B., which in the Cyrillic alphabet is an abbreviation for *"Hristos Voskrese"* ("Christ has risen")—an Easter greeting.

Beat together egg yolks and sugar; gradually, in small batches, add butter, sour cream and *tvorog*. Place the mixture in a saucepan and heat on low temperature, whisking to avoid burning. Once boiling, continue whisking and cook on low heat for 10 minutes. Add the almonds, raisins, dried apricots, lemon juice and lemon zest. Mix well and continue cooking on low heat for another 10 minutes. Remove from heat and cool to room temperature.

Line a colander with a clean, thin piece of muslin fabric or clear plastic wrap. Pour the *paskha* mixture into the colander (this serves as a mold and gives the *paskha* a dome shape). Refrigerate overnight.

To serve, carefully flip the colander on a large serving plate and gently remove muslin or plastic wrap. Decorate the *paskha* with raisins, almonds and dried apricots.

10 egg yolks 1 cup (250 mL) sugar

1¼ cups (310 mL) unsalted butter, room temperature

1 cup (250 mL) sour cream (14%)

6¼ cups (1.6 L) *Tvorog* (see p. 166) or unsalted pressed cottage cheese

½ cup (125 mL) blanched slivered almonds + extra for decoration

¼ cup (60 mL) raisins + extra for decoration

¼ cup (60 mL) dried apricots, diced + extra for decoration

1 Tbsp (15 mL) lemon juice

1 Tbsp (15 mL) lemon zest, grated

MAKES 6 SERVINGS
PREPARATION TIME: 20 MINUTES
COOKING TIME: 30 MINUTES + SETTING OVERNIGHT

NOTE: Traditionally, special pyramid-shaped wooden forms were used to mold the *paskha*, but dome-shaped *paskhas* were also quite widespread.

Cherry *Varenye*

Vishnevoe varenye

1 cup (250 mL) water

6 cups (1.5 L) sugar

4 cups (1 L) fresh sour cherries, unpitted

Varenye is a type of Russian jam, a sweet preserve that can be made of all kinds of fruits and berries. The distinctive trait of the Russian *varenye* is that fruits or berries should remain intact in heavy syrup. This is the ideal way of preserving an abundance of summer fruits and berries for the long winter months.

In a large, shallow enamel-coated skillet or pot, bring water to a boil; gradually add sugar and stir until dissolved. Cook for about 2 minutes and then add cherries. Once mixture returns to a boil, remove from heat.

With a tablespoon, carefully remove the foam, then return the pot to heat and let the *varenye* boil again. Repeat this procedure (removing foam, returning to heat) two more times, then set the pot aside and let it rest at room temperature for 12 hours.

Return the pot to low heat and gradually bring the *varenye* to a boil. Once boiling, remove the pot from the heat, let rest for 10 minutes, then return to heat and bring to a boil again. Repeat this procedure five times.

Remove the cherries with a slotted spoon and place them in three sterilized glass mason jars (about 2 cups [500 mL] each), filling jars up to the narrowing at the top of each. Continue cooking the cherry syrup on low heat for another 10 minutes, then remove from heat and let cool slightly. Pour the syrup over the cherries, dividing it between the jars.

Finished cherry *varenye* has plump intact cherries in bright ruby-red syrup and is best if eaten within a year from when it is made.

MAKES 6 CUPS (1.5 L)

COOKING TIME: 4½ HOURS + 12 HOURS RESTING

Apricot *Varenye*

Abrikosovoe varenye

4 cups (1 L) ripe apricots
2 cups (500 mL) water
4 cups (1 L) sugar
½ tsp (2 mL) citric acid

This great jam can be enjoyed on its own, as an accompaniment to tea or drizzled over blini.

Bring a pot of water to a boil. Carefully wash the apricots, pierce each with a fork in several spots and dip them into boiling water for a couple of seconds, using a slotted spoon. Place them on a flat plate and let them cool down. Cut each apricot in half and remove the pit.

In a saucepan, bring water to a boil, add sugar and stir until dissolved. Cook the syrup for about 2 minutes.

Place the apricot halves in a large enamel-coated pot or pan. Pour the syrup over the apricots, and on low heat, slowly bring to a boil. Cook for 5 minutes, remove from heat and let the *varenye* stand at room temperature for at least 2 hours. Repeat the gradual heating, cooking and cooling procedure 4 more times (5 total). During the last round, add citric acid to the *varenye*.

Pour the *varenye* (both apricot halves and syrup) into three 2-cup (500 mL) sterilized mason jars.

Finished apricot *varenye* has plump intact apricots in transparent golden syrup and is best if eaten within a year from the date of making.

MAKES 6 CUPS (1.5 L)
PREPARATION TIME: 20 MINUTES
COOKING TIME: 20 MINUTES + 9 HOURS STANDING

Cranberry *Kisel*

Klukvennyi kisel

4½ cups (1.125 L) water, divided
1 cup (250 mL) fresh or frozen
   cranberries
⅓ cup (80 mL) sugar
2 Tbsp (20 mL) potato starch

Kisel is another ancient Russian dish that has been enjoyed for many hundreds of years. It is a versatile liquid that can be served as a syrup, a satisfying beverage or thickened a little and eaten with a spoon as a dessert.

In a large pot, bring 4 cups (1 L) water to a boil; add cranberries and sugar and boil on medium-low heat for 5 to 10 minutes. In a small glass, mix potato starch with ½ cup (125 mL) water and gradually add to boiling cranberries, whisking constantly to prevent clumps. Continue heating and whisking until the liquid thickens enough to cover the back of a spoon, about 10 minutes. Remove from heat. Serve hot or cold in porcelain cups.

MAKES 4 SERVINGS
COOKING TIME: 30 MINUTES

MY MOTHER'S MEMOIR: *Kisel*

My grandmother [great-grandmother of the author] always made cranberry kisel *for Sunday lunch in the winter. She poured it out into small but deep little bowls. Kisel looked like a bright red jewel and we would eat it with tiny teaspoons. I thought it was such a prized dessert that I never dared to ask for a second helping, although I liked it very much.*

Nuts in Honey

Orehi v medu

—⋯⋯—

¼ cup (60 mL) hazelnuts, blanched, skins removed

¼ cup (60 mL) almonds, blanched, skins removed

¼ cup (60 mL) walnuts

2 cups (500 mL) buckwheat honey

This is an ancient sweet treat; it's simple yet delicious. In many regions of Russia, wild honey was harvested in the forests by special people called *bortniki*. Their job was to climb high trees in the deep forests and carve out honeycombs.

Place the nuts in a small, clean glass jar. Pour in the honey, cover with lid and let stand for 2 to 3 days. Serve in a small bowl (glass or porcelain) as a side treat along with tea.

MAKES 4 SERVINGS

PREPARATION TIME: 5 MINUTES + 2 TO 3 DAYS STANDING

Gooseberry and Red Currant Compote

Kompot iz krizhovnika i krasnoi smorodini

8 cups (2 L) water

1 cup (250 mL) fresh gooseberries

1 cup (250 mL) fresh red currants, stems removed

½ cup (125 mL) sugar

In Russia, compote is a beverage rather than a dessert or a sauce. It's a favourite in summertime, and especially enjoyed by children (fruit juices are not part of typical Russian traditional cuisine).

In a large pot, bring water to a boil, add gooseberries, red currants and sugar and simmer on medium-low heat for 10 to 15 minutes until berries start to lose their colour. Remove from heat and chill for at least 2 hours. To serve, strain the liquid through a sieve into glasses; serve cold.

MAKES 4 SERVINGS

COOKING TIME: 30 MINUTES + 2 HOURS TO CHILL

NOTE: For other flavours of compote try the following fruit and berry combinations: raspberry and apple, black currant and red currant, apple and pear, pear and apricot or blueberry and raspberry.

MY MOTHER'S MEMOIR: *Gooseberries*

Gooseberry bushes could be found in almost any kitchen garden. Picking gooseberries requires some skill because the bush is full of thorns, but if you lift the branch by the leaves, gooseberries hang down from the branch like little beads. Smaller gooseberries are sweeter but larger ones are easier to pick. They give a lovely tart flavour to compotes and make great looking varenye. Compote from gooseberries is more flavourful and delicate than any fruit juice.

Sbiten

8 cups (2 L) water, divided
2 Tbsp (30 mL) fresh or dry mint leaves
2 cloves
3 black peppercorns
½ tsp (2 mL) fresh or ground ginger
½ tsp (2 mL) ground cinnamon
⅓ cup (80 mL) buckwheat or linden honey

Sbiten was once a very popular street drink. It was served by specialized vendors—*sbitenshiki*. This hot, spicy non-alcoholic refreshment rivaled tea in popularity. However, after the collapse of the Russian Empire it became extinct. Now, there are attempts to reproduce the old *sbiten* using modern technology. These mass-produced, modern versions lack the quality and flavour of the traditional beverage. They are typically sold prepackaged in plastic bottles and are not served fresh and hot, in a teapot, as in earlier times.

This is a recipe for domestic *sbiten* that can be enjoyed at home, or taken along on a walk outdoors.

In a small saucepan, bring 4 cups (1 L) water to a boil. Add mint, cloves, peppercorns, ginger and cinnamon, cover with lid and simmer on low heat for 10 to 15 minutes. Remove the saucepan from the heat and let it stand for 10 minutes.

In a separate saucepan, combine honey and 4 cups (1 L) water. Stir to incorporate the honey and bring the mixture to a boil. Remove any foam that appears and let simmer on low heat for 15 to 20 minutes.

Using a fine sieve lined with a coffee filter, strain the spice liquid into the honey liquid, taking care that no debris gets into the *sbiten*. Heat the honey-spice *sbiten* mixture to almost boiling, and then remove from heat. Serve immediately.

MAKES 4 SERVINGS
COOKING TIME: 30 MINUTES

Tvorog

———— ⠿⠿⠿ ————

4⅓ cups (1.1 L) *Prostokvasha*
(see p. 170)

Tvorog is a fermented dairy product rich in protein that is obtained through the curdling of milk and removal of whey. Its closest Canadian alternative is pressed unsalted cottage cheese. *Tvorog* is usually not salted, its fat content is varied depending on what kind of milk was used to produce it and the texture is also variable, depending on how much of the liquid has been drained. *Tvorog* is one of the staple dairy foods and can be eaten on its own or used as an ingredient in cooking. Currently, most people buy *tvorog* in stores; however homemade *tvorog* is typically of much better quality. Homemade *tvorog* has a very short shelf life so it is best eaten right away or stored in refrigerator for a short period of time (about five days).

The *tvorog* (white solid part, retained in the cheesecloth) can be eaten straight with nothing added, or with some salt or sugar to taste. It can also be used as an ingredient in other dishes like *Vatroushka* (see p. 151), *Tvorog* with Sour Cream (see p. 157), *Paskha* (see p. 158), *Zapekanka* (see p. 228) or *Sirniki* (see p. 223).

The whey can be used as a drink or as an ingredient in baking to make extra tender cookies and pancakes.

Follow the recipe instructions for *Prostokvasha* (see p. 170).

Place the bowl or jar of prepared *prostokvasha* in a water bath and heat, on very low setting without stirring, for about 12 minutes. This will help to separate the milk solids from the whey (*sivorotka*).

Cool to room temperature.

Gently pour the cooled *prostokvasha* into a large sieve lined with cheesecloth, and hang it suspended over a bowl in the sink for about 3 hours to let the whey drip down.

MAKES 1 CUP (250 ML) TVOROG + ABOUT 4 CUPS
(1 L) WHEY (SIVOROTKA)
PREPARATION TIME: 3½ HOURS + OVERNIGHT FOR
PROSTOKVASHA

Kvas

4 cups (1 L) rye bread (approx.),
   cubed
6 cups (1.5 L) boiling water (approx.)
1 Tbsp (15 mL) live yeast or 2 Tbsp
   (30 mL) instant yeast
2 Tbsp (30 mL) warm water
10 Tbsp (150 mL) sugar
8 raisins

Kvas is not only a traditional cornerstone beverage in Russian culture, but also an important base ingredient in cooking. This ancient but still very popular beverage is prepared by fermenting dry rye bread with yeast, yielding a refreshing, light tasting effervescent drink. Commercially prepared *kvas* has been available for decades, but still many Russians prefer to make their own. As with most heirloom recipes, *kvas* recipes vary from one household to another (inclusion of different herbs and berries that add distinct flavours), but the main ingredients—water, rye bread and yeast— are always present.

Slice the rye bread into crouton-sized cubes and dry in the oven at 200°F (95°C) until edges darken and all bread cubes are completely dry.

Prepare the fermentation base (called *zakvaska* or *suslo*) by placing the dry bread cubes into a large glass jar that can hold 12 cups (3 L) liquid. Cover the bread with boiling hot water (fill to two-thirds) and let the jar rest for 2 hours.

In a separate small glass, combine the yeast with warm water, add the sugar and stir. Add raisins for effervescence. Pour this mixture into the jar containing the bread and water, and mix well with a spoon. Top up with more cold water to fill the jar and refrigerate for 48 hours. (Place the jar inside a stockpot as the contents may spill over as the fermentation progresses.)

Once the fermentation is complete, carefully drain the water into another container, leaving the thick sediment of rye bread on the bottom. This liquid is the first batch of *kvas*, ready to drink. The sediment (the *zakvaska* or *suslo*) is the base for making the next batch of *kvas*. Move the sediment into a clean glass or ceramic bowl and set aside.

MAKES 12 CUPS (3 L)
PREPARATION TIME: 20 MINUTES + 2 DAY

Additional *Kvas*

reserved *zakvaska*

1 cup (250 mL) rye bread (approx.), cubed

5 Tbsp (75 mL) sugar

4 cups (1 L) boiling water

4 raisins

The quantities for this recipe are very flexible, make it with any rye bread you have at hand. Sugar can always be adjusted to taste as well.

To make additional batches of *kvas*, thoroughly rinse the original large glass jar and place the reserved *zakvaska* on the bottom. Add dry bread cubes (prepared as above), sugar and then completely fill the jar with boiled and cooled down water. Add 4 raisins for effervescence. Let the *kvas* sit for 24 hours at room temperature then transfer into a clean bottle or jar (again reserving the *zakvaska* on the bottom). Store the finished *kvas* in refrigerator for up to 1 week.

NOTE: Add more or less dry rye bread and water to the *zakvaska* to make more batches of *kvas*.

NOTE: If *kvas* is prepared for *okroshka* (see p. 97) less sugar is needed; if used as a beverage, sugar can be adjusted to taste.

Prostokvasha

——— ❧ ———

4 cups (1 L) organic milk
⅓ cup (80 mL) kefir (see below)

Prostokvasha is a soured milk beverage that does not need any special processing and appears naturally when fresh, raw whole milk separates on the second or third day after milking a cow.

Etymologically, the Russian name of this food—*prostokvasha*—means simply fermented, implying the simplicity of its preparation. This is straight soured milk. *Prostokvasha* is a mix of the upper separated milk layer and the greenish transparent whey (*sivorotka*). Shaken together it was traditionally used in cooking, or as a refreshing drink. It was sweet or slightly sour in taste, depending on whether the milk had a chance to ferment.

In a bowl or large jar, combine milk and kefir, cover with a clean dry cheesecloth and leave at room temperature overnight.

The next day, *prostokvasha* will be ready for use as a refreshing drink or as an ingredient for cooking and baking. It can be stored in the refrigerator up to a month.

MAKES 4⅓ CUPS (1.1 L)
PREPARATION TIME: 5 MINUTES + OVERNIGHT TO SET

NOTE: It is very important to use organic milk in this recipe as regular milk from bags or tetra packs will not ferment properly. Kefir is used to introduce proper lactic bacteria that drive the fermentation process.

KEFIR

Kefir is a fermented dairy product that is obtained from cow's milk. Specific strains of kefir bacteria have to be added to trigger the fermentation process. Kefir has a thick texture, and a specific sour effervescent flavour. Kefir is a very popular beverage in Russia and it is also widely used as an ingredient in cooking. Kefir can be purchased in the health food or organic aisle at most standard grocery stores in North America.

SOVIET ERA RECIPES

HE COLLAPSE OF THE RUSSIAN EMPIRE, war time hardships and many years of instability within the new Soviet republic made colossal impacts on Russian cooking. There were deficits of even the simplest ingredients like flour and sugar. Many pre-revolutionary cooking techniques were lost with the emigration of upper and middle classes and the disappearance of skilled culinary experts. Complex recipes were replaced or abolished (as a sign that the tsarist period was over and needed to be forgotten). At the same time, many old recipes managed to survive virtually unchanged—kasha, *schi* and *kvas* were prepared and enjoyed exactly the same way as they had been for centuries. During the Soviet period, blini and *pirogi* saw only minor changes like simplification of fillings and dough ingredients and cooking adjustments for the new electric or gas kitchen stoves (as opposed to the traditional Russian oven).

Under Soviet rule, a new "modern" approach to food was promoted, which had dramatic impacts on lifestyle and food consumption. Now food was regarded as mere fuel for workers rather than something to be enjoyed. Over the years, this strict practical approach was softened to a great extent and Soviet cuisine became an entity of its own with specialties and delicacies.

In this chapter you will find a collection of recipes that were developed or became widely popular during the Soviet period and are now considered a vital part of traditional modern Russian cuisine. Salad Olivier, Vinigret Salad, open-faced sandwiches with *kolbassa* sausage and borscht are all true classics that you'll likely find on any Russian table, and are all a part of our Soviet culinary heritage.

Setting the Mood

To set the mood you will need a plain white tablecloth, lots of tiny serving plates to accommodate all those wonderful *zakuski* and crystal bowls for salads. Put some red carnations in a crystal vase—a hallmark of any Soviet special occasion. Fit as many people as you can around your table (the more the merrier), and play some cheerful music.

These suggestions are included to help you recreate an authentic feeling of the Soviet Russia.

A FILM TO WATCH: *The Diamond Arm* by Leonid Gaidai is a brilliant comedy that quickly became a cult film and is dearly loved by thousands of Russians.

MUSIC TO LISTEN TO: Songs by composer Alexandra Pakhmutova were all very popular during the 1960s and '70s. Her songs are performed by such famous Russian singers as Joseph Kobzon, Muslim Magomayev, Edita Piekha, Mikhail Boyarsky and musical bands like Pesnyari and Samotsvety. Her songs were often broadcast on the radio and television and are familiar to all Russians.

A BOOK TO READ: Ilya Ilf and Yevgeny Petrov's *The Little Golden Calf* is an adventure story of a crook Ostap Bender and two accomplices who are seeking to steal a million rubles that are supposedly owned by a corrupt secret millionaire. The authors do an excellent job describing the daily life of the Soviet citizens in the early years of the Soviet Union.

FOLLOWING PAGES: *Still Life with Herring* by Kuzma Petrov-Vodkin, 1918. ©2014, STATE RUSSIAN MUSEUM, ST. PETERSBOURG

A depiction of a typical family dinner in the early years of Soviet Russia: two potatoes, a ration of rye bread and a thin herring. This painting was done in 1918, an uneasy period for Russia that changed not only the politics, but the culinary history of the country.

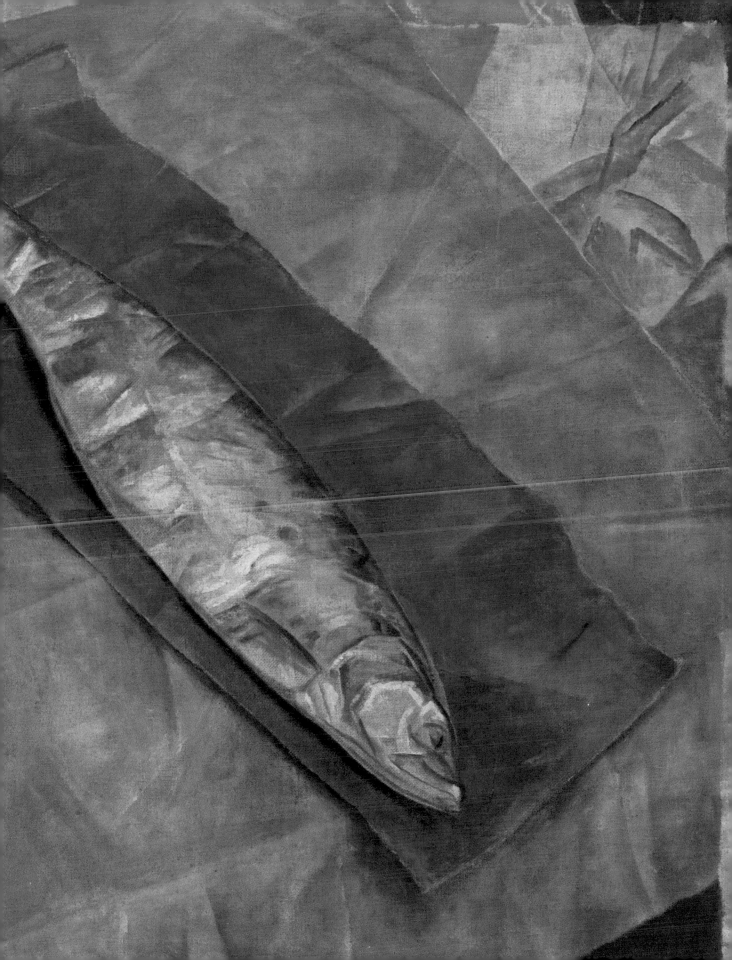

Appetizers

URING THE SOVIET PERIOD, salads became an important *zakuski*. While pickles, spreads, cured meats and fish were still quite popular, the addition of a wide variety of salads brought further diversity to an already abundant range of Russian *zakuski*.

Many salads, such as cucumber and tomato or cucumber and dill, were strictly seasonal and prepared with fresh vegetables straight from the garden or farmer's market. Others, like Salad Olivier (see p. 181), were made for special occasions throughout the year.

Vinigret Salad

Vinigret

1 large beet, unpeeled

3 medium potatoes, unpeeled

2 medium carrots, unpeeled

½ small onion or green onion, finely chopped

2 dill pickles, finely chopped or ⅓ cup (80 mL) sauerkraut

¼ cup (60 mL) fresh parsley, chopped

½ cup (125 mL) canned peas

1 tsp (5 mL) salt

½ tsp (2 mL) black pepper

6 Tbsp (90 mL) sunflower oil

This is a salad made with boiled root vegetables that are chilled. It is commonly served as a *zakuska* and is considered an everyday winter dish.

Place the beet in a pot, cover with water and boil until tender. In a separate pot, boil potatoes and carrots until tender. When the vegetables are cooked, drain water and chill until completely cold.

Peel and finely dice the beet, potatoes and carrots and place them in a large bowl. Add remaining ingredients. Mix well and serve cold.

MAKES 6 SERVINGS

PREPARATION TIME: 1 HOUR

Salad Olivier

Salat Olivye

3 medium potatoes, unpeeled

2 medium carrots, unpeeled

3 hard-boiled eggs, finely chopped

1 cup (250 mL) cooked ham (or boiled chicken breast), diced

2 green onions, finely chopped

2 dill pickles, finely chopped

½ cup (125 mL) fresh dill or parsley, chopped

½ cup (125 mL) canned green peas

1½ cups (375 mL) mayonnaise

½ tsp (2 mL) salt

½ tsp (2 mL) black pepper

This is definitely the most popular of all Russian salads. No special occasion is celebrated without it. The original recipe for Salad Olivier, or *Zakuska* Olivier as it was once called, was made popular by a Russian chef of French origin—Lucien Olivier. He worked in Restaurant Hermitage in Moscow, at the end of 19th century.

The exact ingredients of the original recipe are still the subject of much discussion and speculation. It is believed they were kept secret by the master himself and that Olivier never disclosed the recipe to anyone. However, it did not remain a complete mystery as versions of this salad appeared in other restaurants in Moscow and further afield. The first ever recorded recipe for *Zakuska* Olivier dates back to the late 1890s. This recipe included quail, fresh cucumbers, olives, crayfish, potatoes, lettuce and a composite sauce made with a mayonnaise base.

The salad was well known and always in demand. It is not surprising that attempts were made to recreate the masterpiece at home. Even the political and social turmoil of the revolution and early Soviet period did not diminish people's love for this salad. Due to the absence of many ingredients and the adaptation to the new Soviet lifestyle, the recipe for Salad Olivier evolved over time. Olives and quails were gone, and replaced with simpler ingredients. Here is the current version of the classic Salad Olivier.

Cook the potatoes and carrots until tender and then let cool. Peel and dice them and place in a large salad bowl. Add hard-boiled eggs, ham, onions, pickles, dill and peas. Mix well. Add the mayonnaise, salt and pepper, making sure that the mayonnaise evenly coats all the ingredients.

MAKES 6 SERVINGS
PREPARATION TIME: 1 HOUR

Herring Under Fur Coat

Seledka pod shuboi

1 medium carrot, peeled and boiled

1 large beet, peeled and boiled

1 tart apple, peeled and cored

⅓ cup (125 mL) mayonnaise

1 tsp (5 mL) salt

1 medium onion, diced

1 cup (250 mL) smoked herring
fillets, diced

¼ cup (60 mL) fresh parsley

¼ cup (60 mL) fresh dill

This is a typical modern appetizer developed during the early Soviet period and it is still served on special occasions. The true origin of the curious name is unverifiable but according to a legend it was developed around 1918 by a restaurant (*traktir*) owner. His customers frequently got drunk and got into fights on political grounds. So the restaurant owner developed this deeply symbolic dish where herring symbolizes the proletariat, potatoes symbolize the peasantry, beets symbolize the red flag of the Revolution and mayonnaise dressing symbolizes France, the cradle of the Revolution. The salad was served as a *zakuska* along with vodka and quickly became popular among the customers. They enjoyed the salad, did not get as drunk and got into less fights. The original title was a slogan, and its abbreviated form sounded like "fur coat" in Russian. After a while the political symbolism was forgotten, but the salad with a curious name became a true classic and an absolute necessity on the New Year's Day celebration table.

With a large grater, grate carrot, beet and apple and place in separate bowls. In a deep salad bowl, layer the prepared ingredients in the following order, spreading mayonnaise and salt between each layer: beets, carrots, onions, apples and herring. Chill the salad and garnish with parsley and dill before serving.

MAKES 6 SERVINGS
PREPARATION TIME: 1 HOUR

THE NEW YEAR'S TABLE

The New Year's celebration is a very important gastronomical occasion for Russians, and as any important celebration it also has its own special food traditions. On a classic Russian New Year's table you will always find Salad Olivier (see p. 181), Herring Under Fur Coat (see above), mandarin oranges and champagne. Other dishes come and go, but these items are a must for a proper Russian New Year's celebration.

Mimosa Salad

Salat Mimoza

3 medium potatoes, unpeeled

2 large carrots, unpeeled

5 eggs, hard-boiled, peeled

1 onion, finely chopped

1 can (250 g) Pacific saury or
mackerel pike in oil

1 cup (250 mL) mayonnaise

1 tsp (5 mL) salt

½ tsp (2 mL) black pepper

3 sprigs fresh parsley

3 sprigs fresh dill

This is another special occasion Russian dish. The egg yolk topping represents the yellow mimosa flowers that were typically given as presents to all ladies on Women's Day, celebrated March 8.

Boil potatoes and carrots until tender. Drain the water and cool down the vegetables (for best results, refrigerate for a few hours.)

Separate the egg whites from yolks and reserve both in separate dishes.

Peel cooled potatoes and carrots. Using a large cheese grater, grate potatoes and carrots and set them aside in separate bowls. Grate the egg whites and set aside. Mince the canned saury with a fork and set aside.

In a deep serving dish, arrange the prepared ingredients in layers, covering each layer with some mayonnaise and seasoning with salt and pepper. The layers should be placed in the following order: saury, potatoes, onions, egg whites and carrots. Cover the top carrot layer with minced egg yolks, to create the appearance of mimosa flowers. Garnish with parsley and dill and refrigerate for at least an hour before serving.

MAKES 6 SERVINGS

PREPARATION TIME: 1 HOUR

NOTE: Pacific saury is a type of fish also known as mackerel pike and is often used in Russian and Japanese cuisine.

PREVIOUS PAGE: *Classic New Year* by Evdokia Obukhova, 2014. PRIVATE COLLECTION.

This painting is a great representation of what comes to the mind of any Russian when you mention the New Year's holiday—Salad Olivier (see p. 181) in a crystal bowl, a nice bowl of Vinigret Salad (see p. 179), some mandarin oranges and a bottle of "Sovetskoie" champagne.

Cucumber and Tomato Salad

Salat iz ogurcov i pomidorov

2 large tomatoes

3 large pickling cucumbers
   (or ½ big English cucumber)

1 shallot, chopped

¼ cup (60 mL) sunflower oil

1 tsp (5 mL) salt

½ tsp (2 mL) black pepper

This is my mother's favourite salad. My grandmother used sunflower oil made from roasted sunflower seeds and infused with garlic. This oil gave an absolutely amazing, strong flavour to the salad. As roasted seed sunflower oil infused with garlic is unavailable in North America we use regular sunflower oil.

Wash the tomatoes and slice them in thick wedges. Place them in a large salad bowl. Cut the cucumbers lengthwise, slice in semi-circles and add to the salad bowl. Dress the vegetables with shallot, oil, salt and pepper, stir well and let stand at room temperature or in refrigerator (on lower shelf) for about 30 minutes. This will allow the tomatoes and cucumbers to release their juices. Mix once again before serving.

MAKES 4 SERVINGS

PREPARATION TIME: 40 MINUTES

Cucumber and Dill Salad

Salat iz ogurcov s ukropom

1 large cucumber, thinly sliced
½ bunch fresh dill, chopped
1 small shallot, sliced
¼ cup (60 mL) sour cream (30%)
1 tsp (5 mL) salt
½ tsp (2 mL) black pepper

This is a great summertime salad with a fresh combination of cucumbers, sour cream and flavourful dill.

Slice the cucumber into thin rounds or semi-circles and place in a deep salad bowl. Add chopped dill, sliced shallot and sour cream. Season with salt and pepper and mix well. Serve chilled.

MAKES 4 SERVINGS
PREPARATION TIME: 15 MINUTES

Beet and Garlic Salad

Salat iz svekli s Chesnokom

2 large beets, unpeeled
2 medium cloves of garlic, minced
½ tsp (2 mL) salt
¼ cup (60 mL) mayonnaise or
  sunflower oil
1 sprig of fresh parsley

This is a great appetizer that can be served on its own or as a spread on thin slices of bread. For extra flavour, try adding some walnuts.

Boil the beets until tender. Remove from water, let cool enough to handle, then peel and shred using a large cheese grater. Place in a bowl and add minced garlic. Season with salt, mayonnaise or sunflower oil and mix well. Serve in a small appetizer dish, decorated with fresh parsley.

MAKES 4 SERVINGS
PREPARATION TIME: 1 HOUR

Carrot, Apple and Raisin Salad

Salat z morkovki s jablokom i izumom

2 large carrots, peeled

1 medium tart apple, peeled and cored

½ cup (125 mL) raisins

2 cloves garlic, minced

6 Tbsp (90 mL) mayonnaise

½ tsp (2 mL) salt

2 sprigs of fresh parsley

This salad tastes best a few hours after it has been made—this allows the raisins to swell up and the flavours to blend together.

Grate carrots using a medium-sized grater or food processor. If grated too finely, the salad will become mushy, and if grated too large, the salad may be tough to chew. Place grated carrot in salad bowl.

The apple can either be grated using a large grater, or diced into small cubes. Combine with the carrots and add raisins (reserve some for garnish), garlic, mayonnaise and salt. Mix well, garnish with parsley and raisins, and serve chilled.

MAKES 4 SERVINGS

PREPARATION TIME: 20 MINUTES

Herring with Onions

Seledka s lukom

1¾ lb (375 g) herring fillet, salted in brine

1 yellow onion or green onion, thinly sliced

1 Tbsp (15 mL) sunflower oil

1 sprig of fresh parsley or dill

This simple and flavourful appetizer is a frequent accompaniment for chilled vodka shots, taken before a meal as an aperitif.

Rinse the herring fillet under cold running water. Carefully remove the skin and slice into thick, portion-sized pieces. Arrange nicely on an oval serving platter and top with onion slices. Drizzle with sunflower oil and garnish with a sprig of fresh dill or parsley.

MAKES 4 SERVINGS

PREPARATION TIME: 10 MINUTES

Herring with Onions, top (p. 188); Vinigret Salad, right (p. 179);
Radish and Green Onion Salad, bottom left (p. 190)

Radish and Green Onion Salad

Salat iz rediski s lukom

1 bunch radishes, thinly sliced

3 green onions, thinly sliced

¼ cup (60 mL) sour cream

½ tsp (2 mL) salt

This light and colourful salad was often made in spring when the first greenery from kitchen gardens became available. My favourite type of radish is small in size and red with white tips at the root. They are the first ones to ripen up in the garden. Try substituting sunflower oil for sour cream to add extra flavour.

Trim and wash the radishes. Slice them thinly and place in a serving bowl. Add sliced green onions, sour cream and salt. Mix well and serve chilled.

MAKES 4 SERVINGS

PREPARATION TIME: 10 MINUTES

Cheese and Egg-Stuffed Tomatoes

Pomidori farshirovannie sirnim salatom

6 large tomatoes

2 eggs, hard-boiled

½ cup (125 mL) Gouda cheese, grated

2 green onions, finely chopped

¼ cup (60 mL) mayonnaise

¼ cup (60 mL) fresh dill, chopped

½ tsp (2 mL) black pepper

½ tsp (2 mL) salt

1 clove garlic, finely minced

2 sprigs fresh parsley

This festive appetizer was made for special occasions, such as birthdays, holidays or when special guests came over for dinner. It makes a very attractive looking dish.

Cut off tomato tops and spoon out the flesh. Arrange tomato shells on a serving platter and set aside.

To prepare the filling, finely chop the cooled, hard-boiled eggs and place in a bowl. Add cheese, onions, mayonnaise and dill. Season with black pepper, salt and garlic. Mix well.

Spoon the filling into the tomato shells, packing it tightly. Garnish with some fresh parsley and serve chilled.

MAKES 6 SERVINGS

PREPARATION TIME: 30 MINUTES

Crab, Rice and Egg Salad

Zakuska iz krabov

1 can (120 g) of crab meat, chopped

½ cup (125 mL) long-grain white rice, cooked

1 egg, hard-boiled and finely chopped

2 green onions, thinly sliced

¼ cup (60 mL) canned green peas

¼ cup (60 mL) fresh parsley, chopped

⅓ cup (80 mL) mayonnaise

½ tsp (2 mL) salt

1 tsp (5 mL) black pepper

At one point in Soviet history, the government used colourful advertising campaigns to encourage people to consume more canned goods like canned crab meat. For people who lived inland, far from the oceans, this product was somewhat foreign. Despite this, the use of canned crab meat in light, appetizer salads became a more or less common sight at festive tables.

In a serving bowl, combine crab meat, rice, egg, onions, peas and parsley. Add mayonnaise, season with salt and pepper, and mix well. Serve chilled.

MAKES 6 SERVINGS

PREPARATION TIME: 20 MINUTES

Open-Faced Sandwiches
Buterbrodi

T IS NOT POSSIBLE to talk about Soviet era appetizers without mentioning open-faced sandwiches. It was perhaps one of the most versatile dishes, served as a snack, school lunch, appetizer or tea accompaniment at any time, day or night. They could be plain and simple, or lavishly decorated for special occasions.

For these recipes, choose dark rye breads and French breads (thick soft loaves with slanted cuts on top are best, although baguettes can be used too) that are denser in texture and more closely resemble the bread that is typically sold in Russian bakeries. Cut up the slices into quarters so the open-faced sandwiches are easy to hold and use your imagination and creativity to decorate the surface of the sandwiches. As *zakuski* it is best to serve an assortment of several types of sandwiches on one big platter. You can also try making your own rye bread using the recipe on page 197.

Rye Bread, top left (p. 197); an assortment of
open-faced sandwiches, top right (p. 195); Green
Butter, bottom middle (p. 201); Tvorog Spread,
bottom right (p. 200); sprats (flavorful fish that
comes in tins), bottom left

Open-faced sandwiches provide a great canvas for creativity as they can include a variety of breads and toppings and allow the cook to showcase their food decoration skills by arranging the toppings in an attractive manner.

SANDWICH	BREAD	TOPPINGS	GARNISH
Smoked *Kolbassa* on Rye *Buterbrod s kopchenoj kolbasoi*	Borodinsky rye bread or pumpernickel rye bread	Unsalted butter, thin slices of smoked *kolbassa* sausage	
Gouda on French White Bread *Buterbrod s sirom*	French white bread	Unsalted butter, thin slices of Gouda or Jarlsberg cheese	Sprigs of fresh parsley and olives
Sprats on Rye *Buterbrod so shprotami*	Borodinsky rye bread or pumpernickel rye bread	Small thinly sliced shallot, sprats in oil	Sprigs of fresh dill and parsley
Kolbassa and Cucumber on French Bread *Buterbrod s kolbasoi I ogurcami*	French white bread	Unsalted butter, thin slices of *kolbassa* sausage and thin slices of fresh cucumber	Sprigs of fresh dill and capers
Tvorog and Herbs on Rye *Buterbrod s tvorogom*	Borodinsky rye bread or pumpernickel rye bread	*Tvorog* Spread (see p. 200)	Sprigs of fresh dill
Tomato and Shallot on French Bread *Buterbrod s pomidorami*	French white bread	Sunflower oil, thin rounds of fresh tomato, thinly sliced shallot	Salt and pepper
Eggs on French Bread *Buterbrod s yaycami*	French white bread	Egg Spread (see p. 200)	Sprigs of fresh parsley
Green butter on French bread *Buterbrod s zelenim maslom*	French white bread	Green Butter (see p. 201)	
Radishes and sour cream on French bread *Buterbrod s redisom*	French white bread	Sour cream, salt, thinly sliced shallots, thin slices of radish	Sprigs of fresh parsley

Rye Bread

Rzhanoi hleb

1⅓ cups (330 mL) cold water

2 Tbsp (30 mL) vegetable oil

1 Tbsp (15 mL) molasses

1 Tbsp (15 mL) malt

½ Tbsp (7 mL) salt

1½ cups (375 mL) rye flour (approx.)

1 Tbsp (15 mL) whole coriander seeds

1½ cups (375 mL) all-purpose wheat flour

2 tsp (10 mL) bread machine yeast

This is a home recipe (using a bread machine) for rye bread that tastes quite similar to Borodinsky bread, the most common type of store-bought Russian rye bread. The difference between Borodinsky rye and pumpernickel rye is that pumpernickel is made with an assortment of seeds, while Borodinsky is seasoned only with coriander.

If you do not have access to malt you can instead add an additional 1 Tbsp (15 mL) molasses.

Place all the ingredients, in the order listed, into the bread machine bucket. Choose dark crust and regular bread setting (about 4 hours duration).

MAKES 1 LOAF (APPROX. 8 SLICES)

COOKING TIME: 3 TO 4 HOURS, DEPENDING ON THE BREAD MACHINE

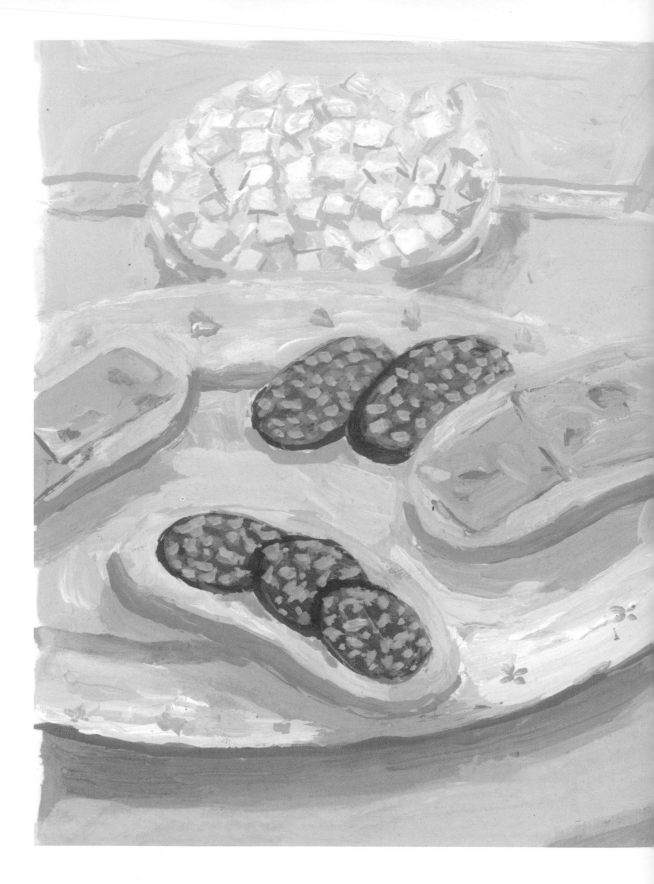

Tea with Sandwiches by Evdokia Obukhova, 2014. PRIVATE COLLECTION.

The artist captured the essence of a quick snack or perhaps a simple breakfast—a plate of open-faced sandwiches and a glass of tea with some sugar cubes. This combination is a common site on the Russian table. Note the metal glass holder for the hot glass of tea.

Tvorog Spread

Tvorozhnaya massa dlja buterbroda s tvorogom

¼ cup (60 mL) *Tvorog* (see p. 166)
   or unsalted cottage cheese
3 Tbsp (45 mL) sour cream
1 tsp (5 mL) salt
1 Tbsp (15 mL) finely chopped dill
1 Tbsp (15 mL) finely chopped
   parsley

Sandwiches made with this spread are a great quick and healthy breakfast option.

In a small bowl combine *tvorog*, sour cream and salt. Use a fork to vigorously mix the ingredients to a smooth consistency. Add dill and parsley and mix well. Spread the bread slices with the *tvorog* and herb mixture and arrange nicely on a serving platter.

MAKES 8 SERVINGS
PREPARATION TIME: 10 MINUTES

Egg Spread

Yaichnaya massa dlya buterbroda s yaycom

2 hard-boiled eggs, finely chopped
1 Tbsp (15 mL) mayonnaise
2 green onions, finely chopped
½ tsp (2 mL) salt
½ tsp (2 mL) fresh ground pepper
3 sprigs fresh dill

This attractive looking spread can be used to make sandwiches that are served as *zakuski* before the main meal.

In a small bowl, combine chopped eggs and mayonnaise. Add chopped green onions and season with salt and pepper. Mix well to form a creamy mass. Spread the egg paste on the sandwiches, garnish with fresh dill and arrange nicely on a serving platter.

MAKES 8 SERVINGS
PREPARATION TIME: 20 MINUTES

Green Butter

Zelenoe maslo dlya buterbrodov

½ cup (125 mL) unsalted butter at room temperature

1 tsp (5 mL) finely chopped fresh tarragon

1 tsp (5 mL) finely chopped fresh cilantro

1 Tbsp (15 mL) finely chopped fresh dill

1 Tbsp (15 mL) finely chopped fresh parsley

This butter can be used as a spread on sandwiches or served over fresh boiled potatoes to give them more flavour. Always use fresh herbs to prepare this dish.

In a small mixing bowl, blend the softened butter with a spoon. Add finely chopped herbs and mix well. Place the bowl in the refrigerator or freezer and let the butter set.

Spread a thin layer of green butter on each sandwich and arrange nicely on a serving platter.

MAKES 8 SERVINGS

PREPARATION TIME: 20 MINUTES

Main Meals

URING THE SOVIET PERIOD, there was an increase in the spread of recipes from one region to another. The government greatly encouraged people to savour the dishes from different republics. This way, local recipes that had been used for centuries were mixed with local specialties from other regions. Public eateries were careful to incorporate specialties from various republics into their menus. Many of these new dishes were eagerly adopted and became new classics, which could be prepared at home using local ingredients. *Shashlik* is a good example of this cultural penetration.

Ground Beef Cutlets

Kotleti

⅓ cup (80 mL) milk

½ cup (125 mL) dry breadcrumbs

1 lb (500 g) ground beef

1 large egg

2 cloves of garlic, finely chopped

½ tsp (2 mL) salt

1 tsp (5 mL) black pepper

3 Tbsp (45 mL) vegetable oil

½ cup (125 mL) flour

Ground beef cutlets remain popular to this day, and are often served with a side of kasha and a salad. You can also use ground pork.

In a small bowl, combine milk and breadcrumbs and let sit for about 5 minutes until crumbs soak up all the liquid.

In a mixing bowl, combine ground beef, breadcrumb-and-milk mixture, egg and garlic. Add salt and pepper and knead thoroughly until all ingredients are well incorporated.

Using hands, form the meat into six flat, oval cutlets.

In a large frying pan, heat up the vegetable oil. Dip both sides of the cutlets in flour, and fry on medium heat until middle is well done and both sides are golden brown. Serve hot.

MAKES 6 SERVINGS
PREPARATION TIME: 15 MINUTES
COOKING TIME: 30 MINUTES

MY MOTHER'S MEMOIR: *Cutlets*

Cutlets were a common dish offered by public eateries and even at schools. A slice of bread with a cutlet was a typical school lunch offered by the cafeteria. Our homemade cutlets were absolutely delicious, and I remember waiting in the kitchen for the very first one—just for me. My mother had a special way of reheating the cutlets on the following day. She would stew a little bit of potato with onions and place several cutlets on top. They would heat up in the steam and give a wonderful flavour and aroma to the potatoes.

Borscht with Beef, foreground (p. 205); Boiled
Potatoes with Fresh Dill, background (p. 217)

Borscht with Beef

Borscht s govyadinoi

1 lb (500 g) beef (brisket) or pork
   (brisket or ribs)

1 tsp (5 mL) salt

1 bay leaf

3 whole black peppercorns

2 cups (500 mL) beets, julienned

2 Tbsp (30 mL) sunflower oil

1 small onion, finely diced

1 cup julienned carrots, julienned

¼ cup (60 mL) tomato paste

¼ cup (60 mL) water

2 Tbsp (30 mL) sugar

1 Tbsp (15 mL) lemon juice

2 cups (500 mL) potatoes, diced

3 cups (750 mL) cabbage, finely
   sliced

6 Tbsp (90 mL) sour cream

¼ cup (60 mL) finely chopped
   parsley

¼ cup (60 mL) finely chopped dill

This lovely soup of Ukrainian origin was eaten in Russia well before Soviet times, but gained wide appeal during this time. Popularized by public eateries and restaurants, this colourful and thrifty dish became one of the most recognized symbols of Russian and Slavic cuisine.

Place the meat in a large stockpot, cover with cold water and bring to a boil. Remove any foam that forms with a slotted spoon, then add salt, bay leaf, peppercorns and beets. Reduce the heat to medium and once the stock boils again remove the foam. Further reduce heat to medium-low and continue cooking for another 20 to 30 minutes.

Meanwhile, in a deep frying pan, heat sunflower oil and sauté the onion and carrots until onion is golden, about 5 to 10 minutes. Add tomato paste diluted in ¼ cup (60 mL) water, sugar and lemon juice, and reduce the heat to low. Sauté until most of the liquid evaporates and the mixture has the consistency of a thick pasta sauce.

Add potatoes and cabbage to the stockpot with the meat. Bring to a boil, then reduce heat and add the sautéed tomato and carrot mixture. Stir, and let the borscht simmer on low heat until potatoes and cabbage are tender, about 10 to 20 minutes.

Once all the vegetables are tender, remove the pot from heat; take out the meat and cut it into bite-sized pieces before returning it to the pot. Cover and let sit for 20 to 30 minutes to let all the flavours blend. Remove bay leaf and peppercorns and discard.

To serve, ladle the hot borscht into bowls or plates, garnish with a dollop of sour cream and finely chopped parsley and dill.

MAKES 6 SERVINGS
PREPARATION TIME: 30 MINUTES
COOKING TIME: 1½ HOURS

Shashlik

MARINADE
½ cup (125 mL) apple cider vinegar

1 tsp (5 mL) lemon juice

2 tsp (10 mL) salt

2 tsp (10 mL) black pepper

2 lb (1 kg) lamb, boneless

2 onions, sliced in thick rings

2 medium tomatoes, thinly sliced

½ bunch cilantro, chopped

½ bunch dill, chopped

½ bunch parsley, chopped

This dish of marinated lamb kebabs became a staple picnic fare and every family had its own marinade recipe. It can also be made with pork or beef.

Mix the marinade ingredients in a small bowl.

Cut the lamb into medium-sized cubes and layer it in a deep glass or ceramic bowl. Drizzle the marinade over each layer. Cover the meat with saran wrap and put a weight on top (a large, heavy plate works fine). Refrigerate for 4 to 6 hours to ensure meat is well marinated.

Divide meat cubes and onion rings among six metal skewers. Grill the skewers over open fire, barbeque or pan fry using a bit of preheated vegetable oil for about 15 to 20 minutes. Make sure the outside of the meat browns nicely and the inside is cooked, but tender.

Serve *shashlik* directly on the skewers, arranged on a platter decorated with tomatoes, cilantro, dill and parsley.

MAKES 6 SERVINGS

PREPARATION TIME: 20 MINUTES + 6 HOURS TO MARINATE

COOKING TIME: 30 MINUTES

NOTE: *Shashlik* can be marinated overnight in the refrigerator and cooked the following morning.

MY MOTHER'S MEMOIRS: *Shashlik*

The most important element of shashlik is the aroma. Someone's first introduction to this culinary marvel usually took place in the open air of a city park. On weekends and holidays, family members took care to dress up and, looking their best, would go out for a walk in the park. It was full of entertainment: carousels (both for kids and adults), live orchestras, pony rides, sport tournaments and boat rides. It was not customary to bring your own sandwiches along so small cafes, ice cream stands, candy vendors and small restaurants were very popular. The king of summer holiday treats was shashlik. Most often it was prepared in the open air directly in front of the customers in long narrow metal trays filled with hot coals. The secret to the tantalizing aroma most likely came from the combination of a simple red wine marinade and the appetites of the people who spent their entire day enjoying the park.

The best shashlik I [author's mother] had was prepared by my older brother. He had just returned from his honeymoon trip to Sochi and decided to cook one of the exotic dishes that he had tried there—the shashlik. Preparations took up the entire day. He carved the wooden spears himself, as they were not sold in stores. He marinated the meat and the onions in young homemade wine. The family was eager to try the new dish so after just a few hours he grilled the meat on pear tree coals that were prepared ahead of time from a branch that broke off one of our orchard trees. It is amazing how simple meat and onions with a new cooking technique and a plain marinade could be transformed into this wonderful aromatic dish. I don't even remember exactly what type of meat my brother used but I do remember that it was the best shashlik that I ever tried in my life.

Pork Cabbage Rolls

Golubci so svininoi i smetannim sousom

1 medium head white cabbage

SAUCE

1 large onion, diced

¼ cup (60 mL) butter, divided

5 Tbsp (75 mL) tomato paste

2 Tbsp (30 mL) all-purpose flour

½ cup (125 mL) sour cream

1 tsp (5 mL) salt

1 tsp (5 mL) black pepper

FILLING

1 large onion, diced

3 Tbsp (45 mL) butter

2 cups (500 mL) white long-grain rice, cooked

1 lb (500 g) ground pork

2 Tbsp (30 mL) all-purpose flour

1 tsp (5 mL) salt

2 tsp (10 mL) black pepper

2 sprigs of fresh parsley

This hearty dish is a great family meal. Usually, it is prepared in large quantities.

SAUCE

Sauté onions in 2 Tbsp (30 mL) butter until they turn golden. Add tomato paste and continue sautéing for about 10 minutes. Set aside.

In a small saucepan, melt remaining butter and add the flour. While whisking constantly, add sour cream and season with salt and pepper. Heat the sauce until almost boiling then remove from heat. Add the reserved onion and tomato paste mixture to the sauce and mix well. Set aside.

FILLING

Sauté onion in butter until softened. In a bowl, combine sautéed onions with boiled rice, ground pork, flour, salt and pepper, and mix well.

ASSEMBLY

To prepare the rolls, blanch the entire cabbage head in boiling, lightly salted water for 15 to 20 minutes. Remove from heat, let cool slightly and carefully separate individual leaves, removing any tough stalks.

Spoon 2 to 3 Tbsp (30 to 45 mL) filling on each cabbage leaf. Roll them up folding edges inside, to form an envelope.

Preheat oven to 350°F (175°C). Place the cabbage rolls in a wide-bottomed ovenproof dish and pour the sauce over them. Cover the dish with a lid or aluminum foil and cook for about 2 hours. Check once in a while to make sure top layer of cabbage rolls is not drying out. To prevent drying out spoon the sauce from the bottom of the pan over the top layer of cabbage rolls. Remove from oven and serve the rolls hot with the sauce they were cooked in. Garnish with fresh parsley.

MAKES 8 SERVINGS

PREPARATION TIME: 20 MINUTES

COOKING TIME: 2½ HOURS

Lazy Cabbage Rolls

Lenivye golubci

1 onion, diced

2 Tbsp (30 mL) butter

2 cups (500 mL) water

½ lb (250 g) ground pork

½ cup (125 mL) white long-grain rice

1 tsp (5 mL) salt

1 tsp (5 mL) black pepper

1 bay leaf

4 cups (1 L) cabbage, shredded

3 Tbsp (45 mL) sunflower oil

¾ cup (185 mL) sour cream

½ cup (125 mL) fresh parsley, finely chopped

¼ cup (60 mL) dill, finely chopped

Though regular cabbage rolls are quite delicious, they are also quite labour intensive. The Russians came up with a shortcut version of this dish. In this recipe, cabbage leaves are not used to wrap up the filling but are instead shredded.

In a large skillet, sauté the onion in butter until lightly golden brown. Add water and bring to a boil. Add ground pork, mix well and bring to a boil again. Add rice, salt, pepper and the bay leaf. Let the mixture boil again and add the cabbage and sunflower oil. Cover with lid and reduce heat to low. Stew the mixture, stirring occasionally.

Once the cabbage becomes limp, about 20 minutes, check if any extra water is needed and add if required (all ingredients should be covered with liquid while cooking). Remove bay leaf and discard. Continue stewing the Lazy Cabbage Rolls until rice is tender, about 20 minutes more.

To serve, add approximately 2 Tbsp (30 mL) sour cream to each serving and garnish with parsley and dill.

MAKES 6 SERVINGS

PREPARATION TIME: 15 MINUTES

COOKING TIME: 1 HOUR

Navy Style Pasta

Makaroni po flotski

2 cups (500 mL) elbow macaroni

1 medium onion, diced

¼ cup (60 mL) sunflower oil

3 Tbsp (45 mL) butter

1 lb (500 g) ground pork

2 garlic cloves, minced

½ tsp (2 mL) salt

½ tsp (2 mL) black pepper

½ cup (125 mL) fresh parsley, chopped

With its minimalist ingredient list, this dish was often made to stretch small amounts of meat and feed a hungry family with a hearty dinner. The first meal that thrifty young housewives learned to make was a pot of borscht, with meat from the borscht ground up and served with this pasta to make a full meal with minimal basic ingredients. In our household, my grandmother sometimes finely minced the meat and pan fried it in butter to give a new twist to this dish.

In a medium saucepan, cook the pasta as directed on package instructions and set aside.

Sauté the onion in sunflower oil until golden then transfer to a small bowl. Using the same frying pan, heat the butter and stir fry the ground pork, minced garlic, salt and pepper until pork is thoroughly cooked. Add the sautéed onions and cooked pasta to the pan and mix well. Let the pasta brown lightly before transferring to serving plates. Garnish with fresh parsley.

MAKES 6 SERVINGS
PREPARATION TIME: 10 MINUTES
COOKING TIME: 30 MINUTES

Kharcho Soup

Sup kharcho

1 lb (500 g) beef (brisket or ribs) or lamb (ribs), bone in, pre-cut in bite-sized pieces

2 small onions, finely chopped

2–3 garlic cloves, minced

½ cup (125 mL) barley

1 tsp (5 mL) salt

1 tsp (5 mL) black pepper

2 Tbsp (30 mL) butter

3 large tomatoes, chopped

¼ cup (60 mL) fresh parsley, chopped

¼ cup (60 mL) fresh cilantro, chopped

6 Tbsp (90 mL) sour cream (optional)

Kharcho is a traditional hearty soup from the Georgia region that quickly gained popularity in the USSR. The original Georgian recipe was often tweaked to compensate for unavailable ingredients. Nevertheless, it was often seen in home kitchens, cafeterias and other public eating establishments.

Place the meat in a large stockpot, cover with cold water and cook on medium heat for about 1½ hours, periodically removing any foam that appears on the surface.

Add onions, garlic, barley, salt, pepper and continue cooking on medium-low heat for another 30 minutes.

Meanwhile, in a frying pan, heat the butter and stir fry the tomatoes until soft.

Add tomatoes to the soup and cook for 10 minutes before removing from heat.

To serve, ladle soup into bowls or plates and garnish with parsley and cilantro. If desired, sour cream can also be used to garnish.

MAKES 6 SERVINGS

PREPARATION TIME: 30 MINUTES

COOKING TIME: 1½ HOURS

Saury Soup

Sup s sairoy

10 cups (2.5 L) water

1 potato, diced

⅓ cup (80 mL) white long-grain rice

1 tsp (5 mL) salt

1 bay leaf

3 whole black peppercorns

1 small onion, diced

½ large carrot, shredded using large
   cheese grater

1 can (250 g) Pacific saury in oil

3 Tbsp (45 mL) sunflower oil

¼ cup (60 mL) parsley, finely
   chopped

This soup is a good example of how Russian people diversified their menu when only limited ingredients were available. It was a very popular soup among university and college students who lived in residence away from home. Canned fish and meats were used not only for appetizers and entrées but also added as main ingredients to soups. This way, one small can of flavourful fish, such as saury (also called mackerel pike), could make a satisfying soup to feed a relatively big group of people.

In a small stockpot, bring water to a boil. Add diced potato, rice and salt and bring to a boil again. Reduce heat to medium and add bay leaf and black peppercorns. Cook until potatoes and rice are tender, about 20 minutes.

In a small frying pan, sauté onion and carrot until onion is golden, about 5 minutes. Add the onion and carrot mixture to the stockpot. Drain any liquid from the canned saury, and add saury and sunflower oil to the stockpot; continue cooking on low heat for another 5 minutes. Remove the pot from heat, discard bay leaf and peppercorns, add parsley and serve hot.

MAKES 8 SERVINGS
PREPARATION: 10 MINUTES
COOKING TIME: 40 MINUTES

Basa Baked in Mayonnaise Dressing

Riba pod majonezom

2 onions, sliced in thick rings

1 lb (500 g) basa fish fillet

⅓ cup (80 mL) Mayonnaise (recipe follows)

1 tsp (5 mL) salt

1 Tbsp (15 mL) black pepper

2 Tbsp (30 mL) water

2 sprigs of fresh parsley

3 thin lemon slices

Mayonnaise (recipe follows) is probably the most frequently used dressing in all Soviet and post-Soviet period cooking. This recipe appeared when Soviet stores began selling saltwater fish in large quantities and people were looking for ways to unite new flavours with usual cooking methods.

Preheat oven to 425°F (220°C). Place onions on the bottom of a greased, ovenproof ceramic dish. Arrange fish fillet on top. In a cup, combine mayonnaise, salt, pepper and water, and mix well to get a runny consistency. Pour the dressing over the fish and onions. Bake for about 30 minutes until a light brown crust forms on the fish.

To serve, decorate with fresh parsley and thin lemon slices.

MAKES 4 SERVINGS

PREPARATION TIME: 15 MINUTES

COOKING TIME: 30 MINUTES

Mayonnaise

Sous mayonez

1 egg yolk

½ tsp (2 mL) salt

1 tsp (5 mL) hot mustard

½ cup (125 mL) sunflower or olive oil

1 Tbsp (15 mL) vinegar

Mayonnaise is a beloved ingredient in Soviet cooking. Its smooth texture, delicate flavour and richness are key elements of many Soviet era recipes. It is often used in salads (including fresh vegetable salads) as a replacement for plain vegetable oil dressing. It is also used as a garnish or ingredient in many *zakuski* and can be added to virtually any main dish. Most often store bought mayonnaise is used, however sometimes it can be prepared at home.

In a bowl, whisk together egg yolk, salt and mustard. Add the oil 1 tsp (5 mL) at a time, whisking and blending thoroughly between each addition. Once all the oil is mixed in, whisk the vinegar into the sauce.

MAKES ⅔ CUP (160 ML)

PREPARATION TIME: 10 MINUTES

Milk and Egg Noodle Soup

Molochnyi sup s vermishelyu

2 Tbsp (30 mL) butter
2 cups (500 mL) thin egg noodles
4 cups (1 L) milk
1 tsp (5 mL) ground nutmeg
1 tsp (5 mL) salt
1 tsp (5 mL) black pepper

This easy to prepare and nutritious soup was a common sight in kindergartens.

In a large saucepan, melt the butter and add noodles, heating for 1 to 2 minutes while stirring constantly. Add milk and cook on low heat until tiny bubbles appear. Add nutmeg, salt and pepper and continue cooking until noodles are tender, about 15 minutes, stirring occasionally to prevent milk from boiling over. Serve hot.

MAKES 6 SERVINGS
COOKING TIME: 30 MINUTES

Eggplant and Tomato Stew

Baklazhani tushenie s pomidorami

¼ cup (60 mL) sunflower oil
2 large eggplants, thickly sliced
3 medium tomatoes, thickly sliced
½ cup (125 mL) vegetable or chicken broth
1 tsp (5 mL) salt
½ tsp (2 mL) black pepper
2 green onions, chopped
2 garlic cloves, minced
½ cup (125 mL) fresh parsley, chopped
½ cup (125 mL) fresh cilantro, chopped

This amazing vegetable stew is very flavourful and can be enjoyed hot or cold.

In a large skillet, heat the sunflower oil and pan fry the eggplant and tomato slices for about 10 to 15 minutes. Add the broth, salt, pepper, onions and garlic and sauté for 20 to 30 minutes. Before removing from heat add chopped parsley and cilantro. Serve hot or cold.

MAKES 6 SERVINGS
PREPARATION TIME: 20 MINUTES
COOKING TIME: 40 MINUTES

NOTE: This can also be used as a spread or served as a *zakuska*.

Pan-Fried Potatoes with Onions

Zharenaja kartoshka s lukom

1 Tbsp (15 mL) vegetable oil

3 large potatoes, peeled and julienned in thick sticks

3 Tbsp (45 mL) butter

½ tsp (2 mL) salt

1 tsp (5 mL) black pepper

1 bunch green onions, finely chopped

1 small cucumber or ¼ English cucumber, sliced

This simple but filling dish is probably the number one comfort food in Russia.

In a large frying pan, heat the vegetable oil, add potatoes and reduce heat to medium. Fry potatoes, stirring occasionally to prevent sticking. Once potatoes become a bit soft, about 10 minutes, add the butter and continue frying until potatoes are golden and easily pierced with a knife or fork. Season with salt and pepper, add green onions and stir well before removing from heat. Serve hot with fresh cucumber slices on the side.

MAKES 4 SERVINGS
PREPARATION TIME: 10 MINUTES
COOKING TIME: 30 MINUTES

NOTE: For a different presentation, cut potatoes lengthwise and slice very thinly. Cooking time will be reduced by about 10 minutes.

Boiled Potatoes with Fresh Dill

Varenaya kartoshka s ukropom

1 tsp (5 mL) salt

6 large potatoes, peeled or 12 small
    young potatoes

1 bay leaf

3 whole black peppercorns

5 Tbsp (75 mL) butter

½ bunch fresh dill, finely chopped

This is a universal side dish that is served with any type of main meat dish. The use of fresh herbs makes it extra flavourful.

In a large pot or saucepan bring 8 cups (2 L) water and salt to a rolling boil and add potatoes. Once water boils again, add bay leaf and peppercorns and cook until potatoes are easily pierced with a knife. Drain the water, remove bay leaf and peppercorns and add the butter and dill to the pot. Close the lid and shake the pot gently to coat the potatoes with butter and dill. Serve hot immediately.

MAKES 4 SERVINGS
COOKING TIME: 30 MINUTES

NOTE: Try substituting sunflower oil for the butter to give this dish a completely different flavour.

Kefir Pancakes, top left and middle (p. 220);
Cherry and Apricot *Varenye*, top right (p. 159–160);
Lazy *Vareniki*, bottom (p. 219)

Lazy *Vareniki*

Lenivie vareniki

2 cups (500 mL) *Tvorog*
  (see p. 166) or unsalted pressed
  cottage cheese
2 Tbsp (30 mL) vanilla sugar
  (see p. 157)
1 egg
5 Tbsp (75 mL) flour + extra for
  dusting and coating
¼ tsp (1 mL) salt
3 Tbsp (45 mL) butter

SIDE

3 Tbsp (45 mL) sour cream
½ cup (125 mL) Cherry or Apricot
  Varenye (approx.) (see p. 159–160)

This recipe takes less time to prepare than regular, Ukrainian *vareniki* (known in North America as perogies), and it tastes great.

In a mixing bowl combine *tvorog* with sugar and egg. Gradually mix in the flour and salt to make a soft dough.

On a clean flat surface dusted with flour, roll the dough into a log about 1½ inches (4 cm) thick. With a sharp knife cut the dough into slices (the *vareniki*) about ¾ inch (2 cm) thick. Dip the pieces in flour and set *vareniki* aside.

In a large saucepan, bring 8 cups (2 L) lightly salted water to a boil. Once boiling, reduce to medium-low heat and drop *vareniki* into the water—2 to 3 at a time so they do not stick together. Once they float freely on the surface, remove them with a slotted spoon and put in a serving bowl, adding bits of butter to avoid sticking. Continue cooking the *vareniki* until all dough pieces are used.

Serve them hot, drizzled with sour cream. Place *varenye* on the side as a sauce for dipping.

MAKES 6 SERVINGS
PREPARATION TIME: 20 MINUTES
COOKING TIME: 15 MINUTES

Kefir Pancakes

Oladyi na kefire

1⅓ cups (375 mL) all-purpose flour

2 tsp (10 mL) sugar

½ tsp (2 mL) salt

¼ tsp (1 mL) baking powder

3 eggs

1 cup (250 mL) kefir

2 Tbsp (30 mL) sunflower oil

½ tsp (2 mL) vanilla extract

3 Tbsp (45 mL) butter

SIDE

½ cup (125 mL) sour cream

½ cup (125 mL) Cherry or Apricot
  Varenye (see p. 159–160)

This is a common breakfast dish, easy and fast to prepare. It features kefir—a common beverage in Soviet Russia that was frequently used as an ingredient in baking (see p. 170). If you cannot find kefir you can substitute plain yogurt in this recipe.

In a mixing bowl, combine flour, sugar, salt and baking powder. Gradually add eggs, kefir, oil and vanilla extract and mix to form a smooth batter.

Heat the butter in a frying pan. Spoon the batter into the frying pan, using about ¼ cup (60 mL) per pancake. Cook on both sides until golden brown.

Serve hot with sour cream and *varenye*.

MAKES 6 SERVINGS
PREPARATION TIME: 10 MINUTES
COOKING TIME: 20 MINUTES

Desserts and Beverages

URING THE SOVIET PERIOD, homemade dessert recipes became very popular. It was a big compliment to the hostess when guests liked her dessert and asked for a recipe. Despite constant difficulties in obtaining ingredients and due to a limited choice of desserts offered by stores, home dessert cooking flourished. Some recipes, like No-Bake *Kartoshka* Cookies (see p. 226), were quite creative, using existing store-bought products as ingredients. Others like Anthill Torte (see p. 227) gave new roles to typical appliances in the Soviet kitchen like the meat grinder, which was used to give texture to the dough.

SWEET SANDWICHES

Quick to make and full of calories, sweet sandwiches were the perfect fuel to provide energy for kids running around until dinnertime or to satisfy sweet cravings.

BUTTER AND SUGAR SANDWICH *(Buterbrod s maslom i saharom)*

This was typical street food, and was especially popular with children who spent most of their time playing outdoors when not in school. It was also served with tea, when other traditional tea drinking accompaniments were hard to find. To make this sandwich, spread some unsalted butter over a slice of French bread and dust with some granulated sugar.

BUTTER AND JAM SANDWICH *(Buterbrod s maslom i varenyem)*

This variation on the bread and butter snack was also quite popular. This type of snack was often taken to work, in which case a second slice of bread was placed on top to make a closed sandwich. When eaten at home, they were always made open-faced. To prepare such a sandwich, spread some unsalted butter over a slice of French bread and spread with any type of *varenye* you prefer (you can try Apricot or Cherry *Varenye* from p. 159 and p. 160).

Sirniki

3 cups (750 mL) *Tvorog* (see p. 166)
  or unsalted cottage cheese
½ cup (125 mL) flour (approx.)
2 Tbsp (30 mL) sugar
½ tsp (2 mL) salt
1 egg
½ tsp (2 mL) vanilla extract
2–3 Tbsp (30–45 mL) butter, melted

SIDE
½ cup (125 mL) sour cream (30%)
2 Tbsp (30 mL) powdered sugar

Sirniki is a rich, sweet type of pancake that tastes very similar to cheesecake. It can be served for breakfast along with tea and an assortment of *varenye* (see p. 159–160) for dipping.

In a mixing bowl combine *tvorog*, ½ cup (125 mL) flour, sugar, salt, egg and vanilla extract and blend well to form a homogenous doughy mass.

Transfer the dough to a lightly floured clean surface and divide it into small balls about the size of an apricot. Press down the balls to form round patties, about ½ inch (1 cm) thick. Dredge them in flour, covering both sides.

Melt the butter and fry the patties on both sides until golden, about 10 minutes.

Serve *sirniki* hot, topped with some sour cream and powdered sugar.

MAKES 6 SERVINGS
PREPARATION TIME: 10 MINUTES
COOKING TIME: 10 MINUTES

Cranberry Mousse

Klukvennyi muss

½ cup (125 mL) fresh cranberries

2 cups (500 mL) water

½ cup (125 mL) + 2 tsp (10 mL)
  sugar

¼ cup (60 mL) Cream of Wheat

½ cup (125 mL) heavy cream or
  whipping cream (approx.)

6 fresh mint leaves (optional)

This light, festive looking dessert can be enjoyed with heavy cream and fresh berries. Add some mint leaves to the garnish for an extra splash of colour.

Place the cranberries in a small saucepan, crush them with a potato masher or fork, add water and sugar, bring to a boil and cook 3 to 4 minutes. Using a slotted spoon, transfer the cranberries to a ceramic or plastic dish and reserve the cooking liquid in the pan. Metal dishes are not suitable as they oxidize the cranberries and give the mousse an off-taste.

Mash the cranberries well and use a fine sieve to separate juice from the skins and seeds. Add the juice to the saucepan with the reserved cooking liquid. Bring to a boil and gradually add the Cream of Wheat, stirring constantly to make sure there are no lumps. Continue stirring and cooking on low heat for 12 minutes.

Pour the thickened cranberry liquid into a ceramic or plastic dish. Using a handheld electric mixer or a whisk, beat until liquid becomes light pink, increases in volume about two to three times and forms stiff peaks. This will take about 12 minutes.

Spoon the mousse into serving dishes, garnish with some heavy cream or whipped cream and mint leaves and serve right away.

MAKES 6 SERVINGS

COOKING TIME: 40 MINUTES

No-Bake *Kartoshka* Cookies

Pirozhenoe kartoshka

two 5 oz (150 g) "Ubileinoe" cookie packages or plain butter cookies

1 cup (250 mL) unsalted butter at room temperature

1 cup (250 mL) sweetened condensed milk

2 Tbsp (30 mL) brandy or rum (optional)

½ cup (125 mL) cocoa powder

Kids often participated in the preparation of this dessert as the recipe requires no baking. Ubileinoe was the name of the most widespread store-bought cookie in the Soviet era and they resemble regular butter cookies in taste and texture.

Grind the cookies into fine crumbs using a mortar and pestle or a food processor. In a mixing bowl, combine cookie crumbs with softened butter, and blend in the condensed milk in small batches (about ⅓ cup [80 mL] at a time). Add brandy or rum for flavour and knead the mixture into a smooth dough.

Pinch off small balls of dough, each about the size of a walnut, and give them an oblong rounded shape, like a small potato. Roll them in cocoa powder and set on a tray. Once all "potatoes" are formed, place the tray in the refrigerator to chill overnight. Serve chilled as an accompaniment to tea or coffee.

MAKES 12 COOKIES

PREPARATION TIME: 20 MINUTES + OVERNIGHT TO CHILL

Anthill Torte

Tort Muraveinik

1 egg at room temperature

½ cup (125 mL) milk

2½ cups (375 mL) all-purpose flour

¼ tsp (1 mL) salt

2 cups (500 mL) butter at room temperature, divided

1 cup (250 mL) sweetened condensed milk

This easy-to-prepare torte was often made as an accompaniment for tea when guests were expected. The hand-operated meat grinder, a typical kitchen appliance found in any Russian kitchen, is used here to give texture to the dough before baking.

In a bowl, mix together egg, milk, flour, salt and 1 cup (250 mL) butter to form a smooth dough. Cover the dough with plastic wrap and refrigerate for 30 to 40 minutes.

Preheat oven to 450°F (230°C). Run the chilled dough through a meat grinder to make long, thin dough strands. Place the dough strands directly on a baking sheet and bake until dough becomes golden brown, about 20 minutes. Remove from oven and let cool to room temperature. Once cooled, break the strands into large crumbs and set aside.

To make the cream, place the unopened can of condensed milk in a saucepan (remove the paper label) and cover completely with water. Cook on low heat for 2 hours. When done, the milk should be light brown in colour. In a mixing bowl, whisk 1 cup (250 mL) softened butter, while gradually adding the cooked condensed milk to make a smooth cream. Combine the cream with about three-quarters of the reserved crumbs and arrange on a serving plate in the shape of a mound—this is the anthill. Garnish with the remaining crumbs and serve chilled with tea.

MAKES 6 SERVINGS

PREPARATION TIME: 10 MINUTES

COOKING TIME: 3 HOURS

Zapekanka

¼ cup (60 mL) butter, divided

3 Tbsp (45 mL) sugar

1 egg, divide yolk and white

½ tsp (2 mL) vanilla extract

½ cup (125 mL) *Tvorog* (see p. 166) or unsalted pressed cottage cheese

¼ cup (60 mL) raisins

½ cup (120 mL) dry white breadcrumbs, divided

¼ cup (60 mL) sour cream

½ cup (125 mL) Cherry or Apricot *Varenye* (see p. 159–160)

This dish is a Russian version of cheesecake. It was commonly served in kindergartens but the homemade version is much more flavourful and delicate.

Using a handheld mixer, beat together 2 Tbsp (30 mL) butter, sugar, egg yolk and vanilla extract. Continue beating and gradually add *tvorog*, raisins, ¼ cup (60 mL) bread crumbs and sour cream until mixed. Separately whisk the egg white until stiff foam appears, then fold in the egg white to the mixture.

Preheat oven to 400°F (200°C). Grease a baking dish (about 6-inch (15 cm) diameter and 2-inch (5 cm) depth will do) and sprinkle the bottom with the remaining bread crumbs. Carefully spoon the cheese mixture (*zapekanka*) into the dish, sprinkle the top with remaining ¼ cup (60 mL) breadcrumbs and the remaining butter cut into small pieces. Bake for about 30 minutes, until *zapekanka* solidifies. Cool down and garnish with *varenye*.

MAKES 6 SERVINGS

PREPARATION TIME: 20 MINUTES

COOKING TIME: 30 MINUTES

Profiteroles

Profitroli

1 cup (250 mL) milk

½ cup (125 mL) butter

½ tsp (2 mL) salt

1 cup (250 mL) all-purpose flour, sifted

4 eggs, beaten

½ cup (125 mL) powdered sugar (approx.)

FILLING

1 cup (250 mL) whipping cream (35%)

1 Tbsp (15 mL) sugar

½ tsp (2 mL) vanilla extract

This was another tea accompaniment, similar to a cream puff, which was made when guests were coming. No-hassle dough and simple filling made a quick and spectacular dessert. Sometimes, custard cream was used for the filling instead of whipping cream.

In a small saucepan, combine milk, butter and salt and bring to a boil, stirring constantly. Add flour, all in one batch, continuing to stir until an elastic dough forms and stops sticking to the saucepan walls. Remove from heat, cool down a little bit then gradually add beaten eggs, mixing them well into the dough.

Preheat oven to 400°F (200°C). Spoon walnut-sized dough lumps onto a well-greased baking sheet (the dough will increase in size about three times so leave enough space around each piece). Bake until dough increases in size and becomes golden brown, about 10 minutes. Remove the tray from the oven and let the profiteroles cool down completely.

In the meantime, combine the whipping cream, sugar and vanilla extract and beat until stiff peaks appear. Cut tops off the profiteroles. Fill the middle of each one with 1 Tbsp (15 mL) whipped cream and replace top. Arrange profiteroles on a serving tray and dust with powdered sugar. Serve with tea or coffee.

MAKES 12 PROFITEROLES

PREPARATION TIME: 20 MINUTES

COOKING TIME: 15 MINUTES

Dried Fruit Compote

Kompot iz suhofruktov

¼ cup (60 mL) dried figs
¼ cup (60 mL) dried apricots
¼ cup (60 mL) raisins
¼ cup (60 mL) dried pears
8 cups (2 L) water, divided
1 cup (250 mL) sugar

This is a great refreshing drink that is usually served cold, but in the winter it can also be enjoyed hot.

Rinse the dried fruits in warm water, then place in a deep saucepan; add 4 cups (1 L) water and bring to a boil. Add sugar and cook until fruits are tender, about 15 minutes. Remove from heat and chill. To serve, strain the liquid into glasses and serve cold.

MAKES 6 SERVINGS
COOKING TIME: 30 MINUTES

Index